The Kingdom of Heaven is Upon You
by C. Matthew McMahon

Copyright Information

The Kingdom of Heaven is Upon You by C. Matthew McMahon
Edited by Therese B. McMahon

Copyright ©2021 by Puritan Publications and A Puritan's Mind®

Some language and grammar are updated from any original manuscripts. Any change in wording or punctuation has not changed the intent or meaning of the original author(s) and has been made to aid the modern reader.

Published by Puritan Publications
A Ministry of A Puritan's Mind® in Crossville, TN.
www.apuritansmind.com
www.puritanpublications.com

All rights reserved. No part of this publication may be reproduced, stored in a retrieval system or transmitted in any form by any means, electronic, mechanical, photocopy, recording or otherwise, without the prior permission of the publisher, except as provided by USA copyright law.

This Print Edition, 2021
Electronic Edition, 2021

Manufactured in the United States of America

ISBN: 978-1-62663-409-1
eISBN: 978-1-62663-400-8

Table of Contents

Introduction 4

Chapter 1: God Reigns as King 7

Chapter 2: King Jesus and Kingdom Proclamation . 45

Chapter 3: King Jesus' Requirement for Entry into His Kingdom 73

Chapter 4: God's Reign as King in Christ's Substitutionary Atonement 104

Chapter 5: God Reigns as King Over His Church in the Word and Sacraments 129

Chapter 6: God Reigns as King in His Final Coming and Exaltation 162

Chapter 7: The Godly Man Loves That Christ Reigns Over Him, Where the Wicked Does Not 191

Other Helpful Books Published by Puritan Publications 217

Introduction

This work is not just about compiling biblical facts concerning the "kingship of Jesus" or "kingdom of God." It emphasizes the practical outworking of Christ's message and intention in taking the fundamental ideas of God's kingdom, (his kingly rule and reign in his kingdom, the proclamation of the kingdom in his preaching, and the response of those to his kingdom being "upon them") that will be considered. It is a study which will point the reader to discern how to live in light of what *Christ* considered the gospel, and how to live before the face of God pleasing King Jesus as a Christian *in* Christ's kingdom.

Is Christ's gospel the gospel we know and love as Paul preached, and many ministers preach today, "For I determined not to know any thing among you, save Jesus Christ, and him crucified," (1 Cor. 2:2)? Is this what *Jesus preached* or *even meant* in his heralding of the good news or the kingdom of heaven? What did Jesus consider the good news, and is it the same as what Paul considered good news? Is the message of the gospel different for the Apostles than it was of Jesus?

Jesus' message in his first sermon was, "Repent: for the kingdom of heaven is at hand." What does it mean that the kingdom is *upon you*, or for that matter, that you must *repent* in light of it? What did Jesus *expect* his listeners to do in hearing him preach this way? How is this kingdom important in light of who Christ is, and what he commissioned his ministers and preachers to preach about him? What didn't Jesus tell his disciples to preach about him going to the cross, or rising from the dead, or ascending into heaven in his exaltation? Or *did* he?

This study will unfold Christ's *kingdom proclamation*, and how it relates to who he is as King, what he does as King, what his kingdom is like, what he considered "God's kingdom" from the Old Testament, what he taught about the kingdom in the gospels, and what the response should be to his kingdom as a result of his preaching. Christ spoke extensively in both didactic teaching and preaching, as well as in his parables about the "kingdom of heaven" and "kingdom of God."

This is not a peripheral topic of study. Christ specifically and emphatically required people to *repent* in light of *the coming of the kingdom*. Much, if not most, of his teaching in the gospels surrounds kingdom proclamation. And, as much as he said that people must repent in light of the kingdom which has *come upon them*, he told them, "behold, the kingdom of God is within you," (Luke 17:21). Is the kingdom within everyone? Is the kingdom only in those who repent? To King Jesus, the kingdom is a *very important topic*. It should be an important topic to all believers. Christians ought to know whether the kingdom is "within them" or *not*, whether they have repented in light of it, and what it

Introduction

means that there is such a kingdom at all! So, *let's get started...*

Chapter 1:
God Reigns as King

"From that time Jesus began to preach, and to say, Repent: for the kingdom of heaven is at hand," (Matt. 4:17).

There are many who think that what Jesus is heralding here is different than the Old Testament or what the Apostle Paul preached later; because Jesus didn't mention certain key truths; that his gospel is somehow different.[1] One does not see in these words here a mention of the infinite God, or the covenant, or the atonement, or the fall of man explained, so, what does this mean for Jesus' preaching? Do such other ideas not apply? He did not come saying, I will one day die on a cross, and you must believe on me dead and resurrected for eternal life. He came preaching "repentance and the good news of the kingdom of heaven." Could it be that this summary statement recorded by the gospel writers, and the intention of the preaching of Christ, and of the kingdom in general, was

---

[1] Religious pundits today try to strip the gospel of its meaning because they are unfamiliar with the word of God in its breadth, and attempt to tear away concepts like Christ's substitutionary atonement, and the doctrine of imputation. In this they show themselves as false shepherds, wolves in sheep's clothing (Matthew 7:15; Acts 20:29), which *destroy* the message of the gospel because of their inability to deal faithfully with the biblical text, and their inadequate understanding of historical theology.

far more elaborate, and far more comprehensive than many give credence to? That does not discount summary statements, it just gives those kinds of statements, context.

Naysayers say there is no atonement, because Jesus did not preach it here. Whatever the kingdom means, Jesus didn't mean what Evangelicalism has always taught about the gospel. They think the substitutionary atonement of Christ was invented later on. But, the kingdom of heaven was not unknown to those who heard Jesus preach; there is a context for them. In fact, Christ knew that the people knew so well what he meant, that the response he solicited was *immediate repentance*. Repentance is very important in Jesus' teaching,[2] and is used more than 2 dozen times by him in the gospels alone.[3] What thoughts did the people associate with this command to repent, about a kingdom, which in Jesus' words, was now at hand?

Here we consider the kingdom of God in the Old Testament. We must look to Christ's bible, the Old Testament, which were the Scriptures he taught from and said were the Word of God, and were those which testified of him.[4] It is in this Old Testament that the

---

[2] Repentance was the preaching of John the Baptist, Matt. 3, and of Jesus, Matt. 4:17; Mark 1:15. Throughout Scripture, repentance is given a center stage, Prov. 1:23-33; Jer. 7:3, 5; 26:3; Hos. 14:1-3; Amos 5:4-6; Matt. 3:2 and is the subsequent condition of God's favor, Lev. 26:40-42; 2 Chr. 7:14.

[3] Compare Matt. 4:17, 5:4, 9:13, 12:41; Mark 1:4, 15, 2:17, 6:12; Luke 3:3, 5:32, 6:21, 10:13; 13:1-5, 15:7ff, 17:3-4, 18:13-14, 24:47.

kingdom is found, and Jesus' meaning of the kingdom is entirely wrapped up in it. The Hebrew noun "kingdom" מַלְכוּת can be rendered "kingdom" or "kingship" in the Old Testament. It is used of God, and his kingdom, as well as used of a political kingdom. "For as long as the son of Jesse liveth upon the ground, thou shalt not be established, nor thy kingdom," (1 Sam. 20:31). A sphere of power of some kind. God's sphere of power is called his kingdom. In fact, "But I will settle him in mine house and in my kingdom for ever: and his throne shall be established for evermore," (1 Chron. 17:14). This is where David is shown to be set over God's kingdom. In 1 Chron. 28:5 Solomon sits on the throne of "the kingdom of God." So even earthly kings sit in God's kingdom, and in their earthly kingdom they have dominion to rule according to justice and mercy as representatives of God's kingship.

God gives power in his kingdom to whosoever he pleases. "And the kingdom and dominion, and the greatness of the kingdom under the whole heaven, shall be given to the people of the saints of the most High, whose kingdom is an everlasting kingdom, and all dominions shall serve and obey him," (Dan. 7:27). In this passage in Daniel is found the succession of human kingdoms until the final kingdom of the coming of the Son of Man which is inaugurated in Daniel 7:13. When this fulfillment of God's kingdom comes, it will be the

---

[4] "Search the scriptures; for in them ye think ye have eternal life: and they are they which testify of me," (John 5:39).

kingdom of the Son of Man, that *divine entity* which comes down from heaven and rules the nations as King, and the church as King.

The kingdom is everywhere pronounced as it is fulfilled in the coming of the Son of Man,[5] the divine Christ. God is king, who is Kingly, has Kingship, and bestows this Kingship and Kingliness on his fellow, the Christ, the Messiah to come, typified by many earthly kings like David. As Jesus preached the kingdom, compiled in this phrase *kingdom of heaven* or *kingdom of God* (both of which are the same with no distinction, where grace is offered to those who need it), the idea surrounds receiving the reality that the kingdom of God is present. To acknowledge God as one's King and Lord, to confess the one God as the King, and reject all other supposed gods, to repent and amend one's ways before the great King is a present reality. To not repent, to not listen to the Christ, is to shun God as King and Lord ("to throw off the yoke of the kingdom of God").[6]

In the prayers of the people of the Old Testament the Kingship of God is constantly found.[7] Often in Jewish prayers God is addressed as *the King of Israel*. Even before they ate meals they would say, *Blessed are thou O Lord King of the universe, who bringeth forth bread*

---

[5] The expression "Son of Man" is one of those phrases that could fill, and has filled, the substance of a few thousand commented books. See my work *Seeing Christ Clearly*, for a full discussion of this phrase.
[6] "For my yoke is easy, and my burden is light," (Matt 11:30).
[7] See, for example, Psalm 5:2, 24:7-8, 29:10, 44:4, 89:18, 95:3, 145:1.

from the earth. This addressed the kingdom of God, and the King in his kingdom. (βασιλεία τοῦ θεοῦ). Earthly figures like David and Melchisedec are seen with royal dignity, as types of the great King of Heaven. Acts 13:21 says that the people, "desired a king;" David being the ancestor of Christ is a divinely recognized king (Matt. 1:6; Acts 13:22). And Melchisedec, by allegorical interpretation, is a type of Christ as the king of Salem, of peace and righteousness (Heb. 7:1-2). But God is the rightful King of his people.

Jesus, the Messiah and King, is the King of the Jews, βασιλεὺς τῶν Ἰουδαίων.[8] The promise of Zech. 9:9, "Behold, thy King cometh unto thee" (Matt. 21:5; John 12:15), is given to *the daughter of Jerusalem* as the true Israel. By divine commission this Messiah King will hold, rule and reign in his final kingdom which is his eternal kingship (Matt. 25:34, 40). According to Psalm 118:26 Jesus upon his entry into Jerusalem is the anointed King who comes in the name of the Lord.[9] Christ is the one who will restore royal dominion to God at the end of the days. It is in this sense described in 1 Tim. 6:15, Paul writing in line with the style of Revelation, where the kingdom of the great King and Lord continues into the ages by the blood of the everlasting covenant of God, and this Messiah comes to rule and reign forever. Jesus Christ is the King who

---

[8] Matt. 2:2; 27:11, 29, 37; Mark 15:2, 9, 12, 18, 26; Luke 23:3, 37; John 18:33, 37, 39; 19:3, 14, 19, 21.
[9] Luke 19:38.

rules and reigns, βασιλεὺς τῶν βασιλευόντων καὶ κύριος τῶν κυριευόντων.

When royal dominion comes by God's Christ, God is described by Paul as, "God the Father, the eternal King." This is clearly expressed in 1 Tim. 1:17, where God is called the "eternal King" of the "eternal kingdom." βασιλεὺς τῶν αἰώνων.[10] The King of the *kingdom into the ages.* As nations are governed by the King, the church is marked by the eternal rule and reign of the King who rules over his people, "Nor by the earth; for it is his footstool: neither by Jerusalem; for it is the city of the great King," (Matt. 5:35). Even in the way Christ taught in the parables God is the King in his varied functions; (*cf.* Matt. 14:9, 18:23, 22:2, 7, 11, 13). The kingdom of heaven is like a mustard seed, a pearl, a treasure, a sowing and reaping, like growing leaven, a dragnet to catch fish, like ten virgins (wise and foolish), like a landowner and a vineyard, *etc.*, for Jesus spoke much of the kingdom.

The Son of Man will send his angels and they will gather out of his kingdom, ἐκ τῆς βασιλείας αὐτοῦ, all seducers and evildoers (Matt. 13:41). His kingdom will finally be pure and holy.

Jesus says that some standing with him will not taste of death until they see the Son of Man coming ἐν τῇ βασιλείᾳ αὐτοῦ (Matt. 16:28), *in his kingdom.* It is a spiritual kingdom as much as its hope is physical.

---

[10] The kingdom which stretches *forever* into the ages.

It is said of the King Jesus *and his kingdom,* τῆς βασιλείας αὐτοῦ there will be no end (Luke 1:33). It is eternal and unchangeable.

Christ the King promises his disciples that they shall eat and drink *in his kingdom,* ἐν τῇ βασιλείᾳ μου (Luke 22:30).

The thief crucified with him asks the suffering and dying Messiah King to remember him when he comes *into his kingdom,* εἰς τὴν βασιλείαν σου (Luke 23:42). A dying thief, one not so well versed in theological matters, knows *quite well* of the kingdom of God and to what it pertains because of his Jewish training in synagogue, and in the Jewish home.

Of the manner of this kingdom Jesus says that ἡ βασιλεία ἡ ἐμή, *his kingdom* is not of this world (John 18:36), not of the *fallen* world. The apostle of Christ attests τὴν ἐπιφάνειαν αὐτοῦ καὶ τὴν βασιλείαν αὐτοῦ (2 Tim. 4:1) Jesus shall *judge the quick and the dead at his appearing,* when his *kingdom comes fully.* Paul knew that his Lord would deliver him εἰς τὴν βασιλείαν αὐτοῦ τὴν ἐπουράνιον (2 Tim. 4:18), *into the heavenly kingdom of peace.* To Christians, entrance is given εἰς τὴν αἰώνιον βασιλείαν τοῦ κυρίου ἡμῶν καὶ σωτῆρος Ἰησοῦ Χριστοῦ (2 Peter 1:11), *into the eternal kingdom of our Lord and Savior Jesus Christ.*

This βασιλεία *(kingdom)* of Jesus Christ is the βασιλεία of God, the kingdom of heaven, the kingdom of God. When reference to the *kingdom of God* and of

Christ is given, there is desired by the Messiah, an immediate response. So that there is a distinction between those of the kingdom and those who try to get into the kingdom which are thieves and robbers; repentance is key in this. The unbeliever has no inheritance ἐν τῇ βασιλείᾳ τοῦ Χριστοῦ καὶ θεοῦ (Eph. 5:5) *in the kingdom of Christ and God*. At the end of the times the βασιλεία τοῦ κόσμου has become the βασιλεία τοῦ κυρίου ἡμῶν καὶ τοῦ Χριστοῦ αὐτοῦ (the kingdom of our Lord and his Anointed, Rev. 11:15); the old world will be renewed as by fire and all that will be left will be the spiritual and visible manifestation of the kingdom of Christ.[11] There is no reference to the βασιλεία of Christ apart from that of God, and God's kingdom as seen throughout *all* the Scriptures; these two ideas are not separated. Christ's kingdom is God's kingdom. This is attested by Jesus himself when he says, "My Father hath made over to Me ... βασιλείαν," *a kingdom*. "And I appoint unto you a *kingdom*, as my Father hath appointed unto me," (Luke 22:29). In this thoroughly *covenantal* concept is the rule and reign of God and of his Christ; that God is king *absolutely*, and ... has a Mediator, who is the great Prophet, Priest and King, who by mediation can reverse the spiritual kingdom of darkness which has come as a result of the fall and usher in the completion of the kingdom of light.[12]

---

[11] "Looking for and hasting unto the coming of the day of God, wherein the heavens being on fire shall be dissolved, and the elements shall melt with fervent heat?" (2 Peter 3:12).

It is God who has delivered men εἰς τὴν βασιλείαν τοῦ υἱοῦ τῆς ἀγάπης αὐτοῦ (Col. 1:13), *into the kingdom of his beloved Son.*

When Christ receives the kingdom from the Father in its fullness, at the last day Christ gives it back to him, ushers back to God its completion as a kind of gift. "Then cometh the end, when he shall have delivered up the kingdom to God, even the Father; when he shall have put down all rule and all authority and power," (1 Cor. 15:24). He can only give to God what belongs to him; Christ owns this kingdom; it is *his* kingdom.

The phrase, *the kingdom of heaven*, which is so frequently and commonly used in the gospel, is taken from Daniel 2:44[13] and 7:14. And it means the spiritual kingdom of Christ in and under the gospel, as it is published and preached to all nations brought by the divine Son of Man. "And there was given him dominion, and glory, and a kingdom, that all people, nations, and languages, should serve him: his dominion is an everlasting dominion, which shall not pass away, and his kingdom that which shall not be destroyed," (Dan. 7:14), which is the substance of the gospel. That's why

---

[12] "...and his kingdom was full of darkness;" (Rev. 16:10). "Who hath delivered us from the power of darkness, and hath translated us into the kingdom of his dear Son," (Col. 1:13).

[13] "And in the days of these kings shall the God of heaven set up a kingdom, which shall never be destroyed: and the kingdom shall not be left to other people, but it shall break in pieces and consume all these kingdoms, and it shall stand for ever," (Dan. 2:44).

Christ is preaching this; what else would he preach, or what else did he preach but the Old Testament, that the reign of the Messiah has come, and it is *at hand?*

This kingdom particularly includes in it, its publication throughout the whole world. Matt. 16:19 says, "To thee will I give the keys of the kingdom of heaven," where John Lightfoot comments that Christ foretold to Peter that he should be the first that should preach the gospel, and open the door of faith to the Gentiles, as in Acts 15:7, and 10. In the kingdom is preached the Christ. All the kingdom is all the work, merit and benefit of the Christ for the good of his people, to those who repent. So, the kingdom signifies not simply the preaching of some form of the gospel, but preaching the kingdom to all men, Jews and Gentiles, with an eye to their conversion, which proclaims the reign of God over the fall. It shows the argument that the lost sheep of Israel must quickly repent, which in turn argues their knowledge of what Christ is saying to them, because the calling of the Gentiles was at hand, which would prove their rejection and casting off, if they did not repent, as Deut. 32:21. "They have moved me to jealousy with that which is not God; they have provoked me to anger with their vanities: and I will move them to jealousy with those which are not a people; I will provoke them to anger with a foolish nation," (Deut. 32:21). The *kingdom of heaven* is understood in opposition to earthly kingdoms.[14]

Does the Old Testament bear this out concerning God's kingship and kingdom? Yes, extensively. "The LORD hath prepared his throne in the heavens; and his kingdom ruleth over all," (Psa. 103:19). "They shall speak of the glory of thy kingdom, and talk of thy power; To make known to the sons of men his mighty acts, and the glorious majesty of his kingdom. Thy kingdom is an everlasting kingdom, and thy dominion endureth throughout all generations," (Psa. 145:11-13). "The LORD shall reign for ever and ever," (Exod. 15:18). "...the LORD his God is with him, and the shout of a king is among them," (Num. 23:21). "And he said, Hear thou therefore the word of the LORD: I saw the LORD sitting on his throne, and all the host of heaven standing by him on his right hand and on his left," (1 Kings 22:19). All the prophets speak about the coming kingdom of God as an essential element of covenantal salvation in the Messiah. "And saviours shall come up on mount Zion to judge the mount of Esau; and the kingdom shall be the LORD'S," (Obad. 1:21).[15]

Consider these elements of kingship briefly, for to *have* a kingdom or to *preach* about a kingdom implies certain important truths.

To have a kingdom implies a king. God is a King. "The LORD is King for ever and ever," (Psa.

---

[14] Lightfoot, John, *The Harmony of the Four Evangelists among Themselves, and with the Old Testament*, (London: R. Cotes, 1644), 138–139.
[15] Compare Micah 4:3; Zeph. 3:15; Zech. 14:16-17.

10:16). "Who is this King of glory? The LORD strong and mighty, the LORD mighty in battle. Lift up your heads, O ye gates; even lift them up, ye everlasting doors; and the King of glory shall come in. Who is this King of glory? The LORD of hosts, he is the King of glory. Selah," (Psa. 24:8-10). "The LORD sitteth upon the flood; yea, the LORD sitteth King for ever," (Psa. 29:10). "And in the days of these kings shall the God of heaven set up a kingdom, which shall never be destroyed: and the kingdom shall not be left to other people, but it shall break in pieces and consume all these kingdoms, and it shall stand for ever," (Dan. 2:44). God is the King of glory, who is surrounded by angelic hosts, who rules heaven and earth in the interest of his people, and receives glory from all his creatures.

To have a kingdom is to have dominion.[16] God will at last actually deprive the worldly empires of their evil dominion and bring in the fullness of *his* dominion. "Thine, O LORD, is the greatness, and the power, and the glory, and the victory, and the majesty: for all that is in the heaven and in the earth is thine; thine is the kingdom, O LORD, and thou art exalted as head above all," (1 Chron. 29:11). "For the kingdom is the LORD'S: and he is the governor among the nations," (Psa. 22:28). "For the LORD most high is terrible; he is a great King over all the earth," (Psa. 47:2). "For the LORD is a great

---

[16] Dominion is the same in this case as sovereignty, but with a more precise view of God's work in relation to *kingship*.

God, and a great King above all gods," (Psa. 95:3). "With trumpets and the sound of the horn make a joyful noise before the LORD, the King," (Psa. 98:6). "And at the end of the days I Nebuchadnezzar lifted up mine eyes unto heaven, and mine understanding returned unto me, and I blessed the most High, and I praised and honoured him that liveth for ever, whose dominion is an everlasting dominion, and his kingdom is from generation to generation," (Dan. 4:34). "And the LORD said unto Samuel, Hearken unto the voice of the people in all that they say unto thee: for they have not rejected thee, but they have rejected me, that I should not reign over them," (1 Sam. 8:7). "But the LORD is the true God, he is the living God, and an everlasting king: at his wrath the earth shall tremble, and the nations shall not be able to abide his indignation," (Jer. 10:10).

To have a kingdom and a king one must have a *throne* on which he sits. "Thy throne, O God, is for ever and ever: the sceptre of thy kingdom is a right sceptre," (Psa. 45:6). "...thy throne is established of old: thou art from everlasting," (Psa. 93:2). "The LORD hath prepared his throne in the heavens; and his kingdom ruleth over all," (Psa. 103:19), the Lord himself being king of the whole world in that day.[17] Daniel saw the "Son of Man" who approached the Ancient of Days on his flaming throne (Daniel 7:9ff). Isaiah saw the Christ on his throne. "In the year that king Uzziah died I saw also the Lord sitting upon a throne, high and lifted up,

---

[17] See also Micah 4:1ff.

and his train filled the temple," (Isa. 6:1). This was the Christ.[18] "And in mercy shall the throne be established: and he shall sit upon it in truth in the tabernacle of David, judging, and seeking judgment, and hasting righteousness," (Isa. 16:5). "Thus saith the LORD, The heaven is my throne, and the earth is my footstool: where is the house that ye build unto me? and where is the place of my rest?" (Isa. 66:1). "Thou, O LORD, remainest for ever; thy throne from generation to generation," (Lam. 5:19). "Then I looked, and, behold, in the firmament that was above the head of the cherubims there appeared over them as it were a sapphire stone, as the appearance of the likeness of a throne," (Ezek. 10:1).

To have a king, a throne, dominion, and a kingdom, one must also have subjects to rule over. God rules creation, people and angels. "And ye shall be unto me a kingdom of priests, and an holy nation," (Exod. 19:6). "He shall build an house for my name, and I will stablish the throne of his kingdom for ever," (2 Sam. 7:13). "And thine house and thy kingdom shall be established for ever before thee: thy throne shall be

---

[18] "These things spake Jesus, and departed, and did hide himself from them. But though he had done so many miracles before them, yet they believed not on him: that the saying of Esaias the prophet might be fulfilled, which he spake, Lord, who hath believed our report? and to whom hath the arm of the Lord been revealed? Therefore they could not believe, because that Esaias said again, He hath blinded their eyes, and hardened their heart; that they should not see with their eyes, nor understand with their heart, and be converted, and I should heal them. These things said Esaias, when he saw his glory, and spake of him," (John 12:36-41).

established for ever," (2 Sam. 7:16). "O LORD of hosts, my King, and my God," (Psa. 84:3). "For the LORD is our defense; and the Holy One of Israel is our king," (Psa. 89:18). "They shall speak of the glory of thy kingdom, and talk of thy power; To make known to the sons of men his mighty acts, and the glorious majesty of his kingdom. Thy kingdom is an everlasting kingdom, and thy dominion endureth throughout all generations," (Psa. 145:11-13). "And in the days of these kings shall the God of heaven set up a kingdom, which shall never be destroyed: and the kingdom shall not be left to other people, but it shall break in pieces and consume all these kingdoms, and it shall stand for ever," (Dan. 2:44). "But the saints of the most High shall take the kingdom, and possess the kingdom for ever, even for ever and ever," (Dan. 7:18). "Behold, the eyes of the Lord GOD are upon the sinful kingdom, and I will destroy it from off the face of the earth; saving that I will not utterly destroy the house of Jacob, saith the LORD," (Amos 9:8). "I am the LORD, your Holy One, the creator of Israel, your King," (Isa. 43:15). There are hundreds of verses this way, about kingship, the king, the throne, his dominion, his ruled people, the ruled nations, and his ruling power.

The New Testament *confirms* what the Old Testament teaches in that God has a kingdom, is a king, sits on a throne and has dominion over all things. "Blessed be the King that cometh in the name of the Lord: peace in heaven, and glory in the highest," (Luke

19:38), speaking of the Christ. The people, "took branches of palm trees, and went forth to meet him, and cried, Hosanna: Blessed is the King of Israel that cometh in the name of the Lord," (John 12:13). "Which in his times he shall shew, who is the blessed and only Potentate, the King of kings, and Lord of lords," (1 Tim. 6:15). "Great and marvelous are thy works, Lord God Almighty; just and true are thy ways, thou King of saints," (Rev. 15:3). "...and the Lamb shall overcome them: for he is Lord of lords, and King of kings," (Rev. 17:14).

Of this phrase, "kingdom" or "kingship of the heavens" or "of God" is God's moral dominion over fallen wicked men as both absolute, and it is particular. The Jewish *Qaddisch* opens with the words, "Glorified and sanctified be his great name in the world he has created according to his own pleasure. May he establish his royal dominion and start his deliverance of his people, and may he bring his Messiah and redeem his people in the time of your life, and in your days, and in the time of the life of the whole House of Israel, with haste and in a short time; and thou shalt say Amen."[19] God's divine kingship consisting in the absolute rule over the whole world, for the good of his people and for

---

[19] Ridderbos, Herman, *The Coming of the kingdom*, ed. Raymond O. Zorn, trans. H. de Jongste (Philadelphia, PA: The Presbyterian and Reformed Publishing Company, 1962), 10. The *Kaddish* or *Qaddish* or *Qadish* is the Aramaic use of the word קדיש "holy" and is a hymn of praises about God which is sung during Jewish prayer services.

the overthrow of any power that opposes his rule, is a central theme of salvation from a human point of view.

That may have seemed like "overdoing it a bit" with so many quotes and Scriptural references. But it is necessary to cite at least *some* of these in proof of the point because of the way the church at large today has either destroyed and misused the concept. Consider that this is a very brief summary of *some* Old Testament passage in regards to Jesus' preaching and what Jesus meant by his use of the terms. In this way the general character of Jesus' preaching of the kingdom has from the outset been qualified as the preaching of fulfillment in the prophetic, historical, salvific, kingdom of God in the fallen world that can overturn the misery of the curse, and bring people into a relationship with the great King; *if they repent.*

Jesus' phrase, "kingdom of heaven is at hand" refers to the government of God as King of the universe who rules from his throne. In the present day many regard the idea of God as *King* to be an antiquated Old Testament notion, and would substitute for it the New Testament idea of God as *Father*. The idea of divine sovereignty must *make place* for that of divine love, so they think. This is thought to be in harmony with the *progressive* idea of God in Scripture. But it is a mistake to think that divine revelation, as it rises to ever higher levels, intends to wean us gradually from the idea of God as King, and to substitute for it the idea of God as Father.

This notion of God as Father replacing God as King is already contradicted by the prominence of the idea of the kingdom of God in the teachings of Jesus. Jesus does not *merely* teach a universal Fatherhood of God at the expense of God as King (as he does in Luke 15 and the parable of the prodigal son). Scripture, overall, teaches the universal kingship of God without exception, as much as it does the Fatherhood of God over his people.

In Psalm 104:1-4 there is a prologue, or a praise of God as king of heaven. In this introductory *strophe*,[20] the psalmist exclaims in wonder at the greatness of the God he worships, clad in radiant light that is implicitly brighter than the sun. Here light is not regarded as a work of creation, as in Gen 1:3, but as an aura of God the King in heavenly majesty.

In Psalm 47, possibly set in its title, it speaks of God's kingship (or enthronement) encouraging all people to loudly praise God as King over all the earth. It begins with an exhortation for all people to clap and shout loudly to God (verse 1), the great and victorious King who establishes his people (verses 2-4). Then it describes God's ascension to the throne amidst calls to praise Him (verses 5-7). Then it describes his reign over the nations and the people of Israel (verses 8-9). God's dominion in ultimate victory is portrayed

---

[20] A *strophe* is the first of a pair of stanzas containing irregular lines, oftentimes in which the whole song is based.

through the common image of God as King in his kingdom on his throne all through psalms like these.

What does God reign over as King? In the doctrine to be considered here in this chapter, there will be two things: God reigns over everything, absolutely (in an absolute sense). And God also reigns over the church, particularly (in a saving sense). Jesus' message is akin to, "God reigns over the fall, his kingdom is over you, so repent." This is the good news, that *our God reigns*. God reigns as King both absolutely as the Royal King over the whole earth, and particularly as Redeemer and Savior of his church.

First, consider God's absolute reign as King over the whole earth. Scripture explicitly declares God's divine kingship to be *universal*. "For the kingdom is the LORD'S: and he is the governor among the nations," (Psa. 22:28). "...his kingdom is an everlasting kingdom, and his dominion is from generation to generation," (Dan. 4:3). Such is the execution of his eternal purpose, embracing all his works from the beginning, all that was, or is, or ever shall be. He rules over the most insignificant things, (like hairs and birds, Matt. 10:29-31), things which are seemingly accidental like casting lots, (as in Prov. 16:33), the good deeds of men, (Phil. 2:13), as well as their evil deeds, (Acts 14:16), — they are all under his kingship and divine control. It is true that God is King of Israel, (Isa. 33:22), i.e. the church, but he also rules among the nations, (Psa. 47:9). Nothing is withdrawn from his government.

Chapter 1: God Reigns as King

In the prophecies of the psalms, of the accession to the throne, God is praised for his kingship. "For the LORD most high is terrible; he is a great King over all the earth," (Psa. 47:2). "Thy throne is established of old: thou art from everlasting," (Psa. 93:2). "Say among the heathen that the LORD reigneth," (Psa. 96:10). *Say among the heathen* that God reigns? This seems odd. Heathen are *lost people*. Heathen are *not* the church. However, heathen are to be *told* that God reigns; they are to be instructed as to the truth of this matter. Not that *Jesus loves them and has a wonderful plan for their life*; that is not the message, that is not the good news of the kingdom *of God's dominion*.

What does it mean that God reigns? "The LORD reigneth; let the earth rejoice," (Psa. 97:1). "The LORD reigneth; let the people tremble: he sitteth between the cherubims; let the earth be moved," (Psa. 99:1). They are to be moved in the heart, soul, and mind to love the reigning King of all the earth, of all heaven, of the whole universe. The heathen are told to do this.

God reigns and rules over *all* in his providence. All the temporal affairs of all things are necessarily in subjection to the Great King.[21] God is the King of nations (against rebel heathens) and God is the King of saints (converted sinners plundered and rescued from

---

[21] God rules over all nations. 1 Chron. 16:31; Psa. 22:28, 47:8; Jer. 5:22; Dan. 4:32; Rev. 15:4. God is supreme and sovereign over all kings. Exod. 7:13; Ezra 6:22, 7:27. God ordains the eternal destiny of both men and angels. Matt. 25:41; Rom. 9:22-23; Eph. 1:5-6; 1 Tim. 5:21.

the kingdom darkness) because God is a warrior, he is the Lord of Hosts.[22] God is the King of angels and Lord of hosts, and is the King over demons, and principalities, and powers, which are placed under the feet of the Great King.[23] And God as King, who has a kingdom, who sits on his throne, who has universal dominion, has a proclamation to make. God has commands for his universe, and the people in it. This is his Royal law commanded to all men. "If ye fulfil the royal law according to the scripture, Thou shalt love thy neighbour as thyself, ye do well," (James 2:8). It is found in his ten words. It is found in the Decalogue The Decalogue is found in Exod. 20:1-17 and in Deut. 5:6-21. God gave the Decalogue to the people at Mount Sinai (Exod. 20:1-17) after demonstrating his kingship in saving them and leading them out of Egypt against the wicked king. Moses then repeated it in his sermon over 40 years later (Deut. 5:6-21). The formulation in the Decalogue is unqualified. God as king imposes demands "thou shalt/shalt not" on his subjects. God absolutely rules as King over all rational creatures in this way, and commands who he wills. This all falls under his universal dominion and reign as King. Yet, these commandments also represent the minimum moral and religious requirements for those in covenant relationship with God, which are directed at

---

[22] See Jeremiah Burroughs' work, *The Glorious Name of God the Lord of Hosts* published by Puritan Publications for a full discussion of that excellent designation and title of God.
[23] Psa. 103:20-21; Job 1:12.

Chapter 1: God Reigns as King

individuals as members of the everlasting covenant *of the Christ*, who is the lawgiver and King.

Consider, now, the particular rule of God. God's particular reign as King is by covenant. Yes, he rules by covenant. He says, "And *I will put enmity* between thee and the woman, and between thy seed and her seed; it shall bruise thy head, and thou shalt bruise his heel," (Genesis 3:15), the King speaks and commands these things concerning the fall, and can command salvation from the fall.[24] God *will put* enmity? God does this? Yes, because God's dominion covers all things, for Christ in subduing his church to himself, in ruling and defending them, and in restraining and conquering all his and their enemies is the Great King. The coming divine manifestation of the King of heaven, holds forth the rule of the Messiah-King over all things, especially the fall. In the explanation of the dream to Daniel it is said that it is, "the saints of the Most High who shall take the kingdom and possess it for ever," (Dan. 7:18).

In Zechariah, God rules the world by the ministry of angels, in the vision of the four chariots (Zech. 6:1–8), messengers who are sent out to proclaim his kingship. God, as King of saints, ruling the church by the mediation of Christ, in the figure of Joshua the high priest crowned, the ceremony performed, and then explained concerning the coming of the Christ (Zech. 6:9–15). "And speak unto him, saying, Thus speaketh

---

[24] *cf.* Num. 23:21; Judges 8:23; 1 Sam. 8:7; 12:12; Psa. 48:3; Isa. 41:21; Jer. 8:19; Micah 2:13; also Exod. 19:6.

the LORD of hosts, saying, Behold the man whose name is The BRANCH; and he shall grow up out of his place, and he shall build the temple of the LORD," (Zech. 6:12). What is this temple of the Lord? "Even he shall build the temple of the LORD; and he shall bear the glory, and shall sit and rule upon his throne; and he shall be a priest upon his throne," (Zech. 6:13). He is both King and Priest on his throne. It is only through his Messiah that God particularly rules his people, to take off their dirty garments, and give them white robes as he did with Joshua.

God's reign as King is very *particular* through his Messiah. What this means is that, it is *God as King through the Christ over the fall* in his rule. Salvation in light of the fall requires God to be King over the fall, because without his power to reverse it, there would be no reigning over it. What would he be able to change about the fall, to put to death sin, to put to death the deeds of the sinful man by the Spirit, if he had no power to do so? He is the church's all-powerful, true spiritual King (Deut. 33:5; 1 Sam. 12:12; 1 Chron. 17:14; 28:5), able to command the heart in his spiritual reign over men's hearts. God intimately involves himself in the control and direction of the church's destiny through the enthroned Messiah. Ezekiel saw this Messiah enthroned on his movable chariot at the River Chebar (Ezekiel 1:1). He is found in every place, and rules on his throne everywhere.[25] Isaiah saw this Messiah high and

---

[25] "...the likeness of a throne," (Ezek. 1:26).

lifted up on his throne (Isa. 6:1-4), where even the most insignificant parts of his robe, his *high priestly robes*, the bells and pomegranates dangling on his hem, filled the temple, of sweetness and service in his rule and reign. Daniel saw this Messiah in the courtroom of the Ancient of Days in Daniel 7. There he is found in the law court of the Most High ruling over the thoughts, deeds, actions, hearts of men, opening the books recorded for all time, and bringing just judgment against all. Christ is "Head over everything for the church, *which is his body*," (Eph. 1:22–23), this italicized phrase is a parallel to the Old Testament emphasis. The rule of God extends over all—but finds special focus in his concern for his church, *which is his body*. All the types and shadows of the Old Testament are bound up in the dominion of God over the fall that the Messiah has come and fulfilled his covenant obligations, and in so doing put an end to the reign of death. He will make his body glorious ... he will make his bride glorious. He will one day set up an everlasting kingdom on earth, and the spiritual rule of the church;[26] one day it will be seen in its fullness, where the dimensions of earth and heaven coalesce. Daniel and Isaiah added their descriptions: the King will be God, and yet of David's line. When the Messiah comes, the rule of God will find visible and overwhelming expression as God openly exercises his once-hidden power that was cloaked in types and shadows. It was a version of this kingdom the Jews

---

[26] Isa. 24:23; Micah 4:6; Zech. 14:9–17.

expected and yearned for. And it was this kingdom which is described in the prophecies which the Apostle Matthew relates about Jesus. But the Jews thought it was merely earthly. There is no doubt what Jesus' listeners pictured in their minds when Jesus announced the good news that the kingdom was at hand. They were looking for a *physical world domination* by God's Messiah. His orthodox listeners were sure he meant the end times expression of the rule of God. But they thought "kingdom of heaven" must mean God's revelation of his power and goodness through Messiah's righteous, endless rule over the temporary *right now*. They were thinking, "Get rid of these Roman oppressors!" They were, indeed, small minded in this. Such a rule is so much bigger than a revolt against a fading empire. They missed that this spiritual rule, this particular rule is set in the context of repentance in light of the kingdom.

God as King desires the sinner's initial, fundamental and universal repentance, (Ezek. 18:23, 33:11, 18:31-32). He commands it, (Acts 17:30; Mark 1:14-15). He invites to it, (Isa. 1:16, *etc.*, and 55:7; Matt. 3:2; Ezek. 18:23, 31-32; Jer. 3:1). He promises great saving blessings and benefits to the penitent, (Isa. 55:7; Zech. 1:3; Acts 2:38; Hos. 14:1-4; Ezek. 18:21-22; Acts 26:18). He says to his people he has, "no pleasure in the death of the sinner, but that he should repent and live," (Ezek. 18:23, 33:11). He gladly receives sinners who repent, (Luke 15:3ff). Jesus' first sermon was of *repentance,* (Matt. 4:17; Mark 1:1-15), and he immediately required all who heard his preaching to repent, because they were *very familiar* with kingdom concepts; and by saying the *kingdom* is present, demonstrated that he was the One who would usher it in, which attested to his divinity; and ultimately, this is why they crucified him.[27]

The time of the Messiah coming in the flesh is fulfilled in the Christ, and the kingdom of God, the Messiah's kingdom, is at hand. In fact, it is to Christians today, already at hand. It has already come. All should repent and yield obedience to Messiah the Prince, to Messiah the King. Why should they repent and yield obedience to the King's laws? That they may be suitable and tempered for the reception of God's Kingly Christ, and of his kingdom, to their salvation in their heart, soul and mind. This has happened so that they might gladly render him a King's service.

There are two important points in light of the coming of the kingdom in this. First, there is a judgment motif in view of looking at the coming of the kingdom as it applies to the end times (eschatologically). In Matthew 4:17 the eschatological idea is stated in this way, "Repent, for the kingdom of heaven is at hand." Judgment, even eschatological judgment (end time judgment), is directly connected with eternal concepts, as in Hebrews 9:27, "And as it is

---

[27] "Therefore the Jews sought the more to kill him, because he not only had broken the sabbath, but said also that God was his Father, making himself equal with God," (John 5:18).

appointed for men to die once, but after this the judgment." One day, like the unjust steward,[28] the books will be required of every man, for *the kingdom is at hand*. Every person is going to have to turn in their books and give an account, now when they die and then at his coming, for the kingdom of heaven is at hand, and God rules from his throne and commands of men certain things they must comply with, or ... face the wrath of the Great King.[29]

The Covenant of Works in the garden with Adam did not allow for any kind of repentance. It caused all things in its failure of being upheld by knowledgeable, holy and righteous Adam, to be instantly *damned*. And everyone, now, that cannot perform in their own strength perfect and personal obedience to the Great King, is *damned, i.e.* fallen and under the coming judgment and the justice of God. Repentance only comes by way of the Covenant of Grace, which is what Jesus *is* preaching. Such only comes in by the gospel, the good news, that *our God reigns*, and everything attached to that Old Testament idea of being born again is realized in that phrase. The good news that men are not left in misery and cursedness, but instead, *our God reigns*, he sits on his throne and rules over everything. He rules absolutely everything, *especially the curse* in light of salvation,

---

[28] Luke 16.
[29] "For which things' sake the wrath of God cometh on the children of disobedience," (Col. 3:6).

particularly able to reverse the fall so that men may come before the throne, and bow to touch his golden scepter which he holds out to them. "...and the king held out to Esther the golden sceptre that was in his hand. So Esther drew near, and touched the top of the sceptre," (Esther 5:2). By the fruit of the work of Messiah the Prince, God as King rules the fall and embodied in this is all that comprises his gracious covenant, all that encompasses God's kingly rule over the world, and his covenant rule over his church.[30]

There is another point to be made, and that concerns Christ's Kingly dominion over the Fall. It is very good news that that men can be saved by the great King. Who shall save them? Christ the King shall save them. How shall he save them? By his rule and reign. How is this done? His rule and reign are accomplished and enacted in his work and merit of perfect holiness.

God's dominion is manifested in his law and in his will. I have said this many times, *no holiness, no heaven*; we might take this to mean in Christ's preaching, *no immediate repentance, then no salvation*. How will the King of heaven, in his kingdom which is at God's right hand, and who offers to stretch out the golden scepter by way of repentance, treat men who *despise* his kingly rule? His rule and reign are nothing else but his own will enforced. God first gave a positive law to Adam of, "not eating of the tree of knowledge of good and evil," (Gen.

---

[30] See the 1647 *Westminster Confession of Faith*, chapter 7 on *covenant*.

2:17),[31] which was to be Adam's assent to God's asserted dominion over him. God shows himself the King and Lord of man, and that Adam was simply to be a *steward* of the King, reflecting the King's laws. God's kingly dominion is set in his laws, and his majesty is seen in publishing his laws.[32] All this is bound up in the phrase, "the kingdom of heaven is at hand," so... repent, which is what the Christ says of his own rule. Though men can be saved, and God can reverse the fall, there is an obligation to demonstrate one's allegiance to King Jesus. The King's law pierces the soul and reaches into the conscience. Good stewards of the law, cannot add to it, can cannot take away from it. What a most horrid thought of so many today, that do not uphold the kingdom as God has given it and reject the law of God. They remove the law, change his worship, reject his statues, and what will the King think of these people who do such things and abuse such things which are given to reverse the fall ... if they are used as the Great King prescribes? The King in his sovereignty will appear and punish all transgressors of his law. Exod. 17:16 says, "The Lord hath sworn, that the Lord will have war," the Hebrew is more literally, "The hand upon the throne of the Lord," as a "lawgiver" he "saves or destroys" as also James 4:12 echoes. The King will not trifle with the lawbreakers as lawbreakers trifle

---

[31] This was a negative statement (which comprises the "not" of the verse) but a positive rule for holiness.
[32] See Exodus 20:1-2.

with his kingdom. The psalmist says, the majesty of God's kingdom is accomplished in "righteousness and judgment" which "are the habitation of his throne," (Psalm 97:1-2), and he is very serious as King about such things.

Christ, the Messiah, shows himself as this King who can reverse the law by preaching about the "how" of reversing it. How? *Our God Reigns.* He reigns in the kingdom of heaven. His kingdom appears in its covenant as God enthroned absolutely and particularly. How does he do this, but through his reign as Messiah, in fulfillment of his covenant obligations between the Father, Son and Spirit in the Covenant of Redemption. This little phrase, "kingdom of God" "kingdom of heaven" comprises all God does in reversing the fall, and so the necessary outcome is to repent in light of it, as it contains everything about his eternal and everlasting covenant. Repent in light of God's kingly ability and power to bestow grace wheresoever he wills through the Christ's work and merit by faith alone; do this through what God provides to make satisfaction for sinners to come into a right relationship with him through kingdom repentance.

Men have no ability to save themselves.[33] The very phrases *kingdom of God, kingdom of heaven* show there is no strength in men to climb out of the hole of the curse; the *kingdom of man* is a terrible kingdom, filled

---

[33] "And you hath he quickened, who were dead in trespasses and sins," (Eph. 2:1).

with darkness and sin, and to reverse the fall in Christ's reign is God's prerogative, and kingly compassion on those he sees as miserable to receive mercy.[34]

Christ does not save by any obligation; he is King. He is indebted to no one but the Father by a voluntary covenant, and the Spirit, in fulfilling all that he must as Surety, which he *promised* to do as the King.[35] No one deserves the King's grace, which is why it is called *grace and mercy*. His power and reigning authority over the fall to change them. Such is an act merely of his Kingly beneficence as the Christ. The dominion of the Christ manifests its glory among men by defeating the purposes and devices of the devil and death; things which hold men in bondage to sin. The dominion of the great reigning King disposes of the lives of men in whichever way he pleases, but he is especially pleased to save them, and hold out his golden scepter that they may be converted. He holds the keys of death and hell in his own hand, and may bestow it in his kingship on whom he desires; and will reject none that come to him by faith.

---

[34] "Thus saith the LORD; Cursed be the man that trusteth in man, and maketh flesh his arm, and whose heart departeth from the LORD," (Jer. 17:5).

[35] "Even he shall build the temple of the LORD; and he shall bear the glory, and shall sit and rule upon his throne; and he shall be a priest upon his throne: and the counsel of peace shall be between them both," (Zech. 6:13). "...who for the joy that was set before him endured the cross, despising the shame, and is set down at the right hand of the throne of God," (Heb. 12:2).

The *whole gospel* is built on this: the kingdom of heaven is at hand: as it is so said in Scripture, *Our God Reigns*, and he reigns over the fall by Messiah the Prince; for Christ is the Prince of Peace and Mighty God, and King, and can reverse the fall in those who he gifts with repentance.[36] God, in his kingly power appears in appointing Christ to fulfill this gospel, this work of redemption. And this Christ, by God's kingly command, whom God created all things, not only became God with us, but a crucified man, by the will of his Father (Gal. 1:4), "who gave himself for our sins according to the will of God." He was the eternal Son by nature, and Mediator of God's covenant, by divine will. "Lo, I come; I delight to do thy will," (Heb. 10:7), "Lo, I come to do thy will, O God." The covenant of Christ to accomplish this work was an act of mercy, founded on the rule and reign of the King on his throne.

God's kingly rule and dominion are seen over the fall in transferring a sinner's sins on Christ as they believe by faith in the work of the crucified Messiah; this is the heart of God's reigning in men. Isa. 53:6 says, "The Lord hath laid upon him the iniquity of us all." "He hath made him to be sin for us," (2 Cor. 5:21). He was made so by the fall reversing power and delight of the King in his sovereign pleasure to make him an offering for the sin of his people.

---

[36] "...if God peradventure will give them repentance to the acknowledging of the truth," (2 Tim. 2:25).

This is why Christ is the King, because he is exalted to the right hand as God's fellow, and *he is God.* Matt. 28:28, "All power is given me." Do you think he said such things lightly? And he, "gave him to be head over all things to the church," (Eph. 1:22). "God gave him a name above every name" (Phil. 2:9), that name is LORD; and, therefore, he sits upon the throne called, "the throne of his Father," (Rev. 3:21). Ezek.37:24-25 says, "David, my servant, shall be king over them," and "my servant David shall be their prince forever." There the rule of God's reigning is seen in Christ as the great Prophet, Priest and King of his people, the Spiritual David to rescue his sheep from the mouth of lion and the paw of the bear.[37]

The King requires your obedience in his absolute and particular reign, regardless of whether you are sinner or saint. God rules and reigns, and sits high and lofty above you. He rules over you and reigns over you. Acknowledge it or not, it does not negate the reality that the King rules, and he requires your compliance to his kingly dominion. Those who do not repent, those who do not comply, are cast into outer darkness in the end,[38] for they deserve the same future that the devil, whom they follow, does. Inwardly they

---

[37] "David said moreover, The LORD that delivered me out of the paw of the lion, and out of the paw of the bear, he will deliver me out of the hand of this Philistine. And Saul said unto David, Go, and the LORD be with thee," (1 Sam. 17:37).

[38] "...shall be cast out into outer darkness: there shall be weeping and gnashing of teeth," (Matt. 8:12).

serve the devil and do the desires of their father. They inwardly do not serve King Jesus on his throne if they are still in the kingdom of darkness. There are some people who may outwardly serve him, even if unknowingly; for God has raised up such people to serve him even in their rebellion against him. But, those who are made able to comply render service to God that is acceptable because they are transformed by the King, and what should you be thinking about this?

Your obedience must be exact and sincere to the Great King; not negligent. Christ as King calls for the highest service and worship from you. He is the Great King, and he must gain from you, not lame sacrifices, but those perfect ones, of heart, soul and mind, covered in the blood of the Savior. Obedience is due to him as King for this great salvation, for he will receive nothing less, because he is the most excellent King.[39] You are compelled to obey him by his word in this.

You must sincerely love him with an exclusive obedience as the Great King commands, without reservation and that, continually. He commands you to obey with a full heart, with a full soul and with a full mind, Matt. 4:10 says, "Him only shalt thou serve." To do anything other is to serve God by halves, to serve him in part, which is not to serve him at all, as all those Jehu-like are cast off.[40]

---

[39] "...present your bodies a living sacrifice, holy, acceptable unto God, which is your reasonable service," (Rom. 12:1).

Your obedience to the Great King must be universal obedience which answers to his absolute rule.[41] You are, in all places, at all times, answerable to the King who is over you *in all places at all times*. Are you ready with acceptable service because you love him? And this service, which is a test of a true Christian, is to be done by you while rejoicing in the Great King. He commands your attitude as much as your body. He is King over how you think, feel and act, his laws cover such. There is no wedge of gold to be kept back for yourself. There is no Babylonish garment that you keep like Achan did.[42] Instead, Psalm 119:24, "Thy testimonies ... are my delight."

The King is a delight to serve. Is it delightful to you to serve the Great King? Is it delightful to serve the King always? That's a different question for you if you are a saint or sinner. Sinners hate to comply, they long and try to do their own thing. Saints desire to comply, because they love the King and what he has done for them. "Yes," you might say, "it is a delight to be saved

---

[40] "But Jehu took no heed to walk in the law of the LORD God of Israel with all his heart: for he departed not from the sins of Jeroboam, which made Israel to sin," (2 Kings 10:31).

[41] *Westminster Larger Catechism*, Question 1: What is the chief and highest end of man? Answer 1: Man's chief and highest end is to glorify God, and fully to enjoy him forever, (Rom. 11:36; 1 Cor. 10:31; Psa. 73:24-28).

[42] "But the children of Israel committed a trespass in the accursed thing: for Achan, the son of Carmi, the son of Zabdi, the son of Zerah, of the tribe of Judah, took of the accursed thing: and the anger of the LORD was kindled against the children of Israel," (Joshua 7:1).

by the God who reigns over the fall through the Christ and has saved me; what a sweet gospel it is to my mind." And yet, is it perpetually a delight to you? Is the good news that *Our God Reigns*, that our God is the Great King over your life, is this always good news to you? You say, "Oh, yes, no matter what." Is it a delight in sickness? Is it a delight in affliction or turmoil or calamity? Is it only a delight in things you find delightful? A King will require at his servant's hands, all kinds of due obedience to his wishes. Service to Christ is to be done in compliance with all God's directives, statues, precepts, commands and laws.

God requires that your obedience here on earth is as fit as if it was done in heaven, done before the very throne of the Christ, because all that happens on earth is done before the very throne of the Great King. In heaven God's will is done perfectly by the angels and saints there.[43] On earth it is to be the same by you. Is this not what you pray daily, "thy will be done on earth as it is in heaven?" Do you mean what you pray? His kingdom is of power, and glory, forever, holding forth the keys of death and hell, and yet Jesus does not preach "the kingdom of Hell is upon you," but rather, the kingdom of heaven is held out, and you are to render obedience to that sweet kingdom of rule and grace. Devils, reprobates, *everyone* bows to this kingdom passively now, even if they do not acknowledge it. Yet, there are also the good angels and those who are elect

---

[43] "Thy will be done in earth, as it is in heaven," (Matt. 6:10).

which actively desire to serve the king *now* before his holy throne. It does not matter if the wicked say "Christ shall not reign over me," because at the judgment he will have them all bow to him, and they will call him Lord, *especially* the evil angels, the devil, and the wicked.[44] He will make sinners comply at first sight, because they will be compelled by seeing the Great King seated on the throne in his Kingship which they will not deny, and have no excuse from not bearing obedience to his will while they lived here on this terrestrial ball seeing his great glory. They will know it, and they will both fear him, and despise him for it; but render not a single excuse against it.[45]

But you bowing to the King now by grace through faith in holy service is a means to glorify his gospel, by which he reigns over you in reversing the fall in you; he does this through the Savior, by the condition of repentance. Is that the constant condition of your own life? It is a kingdom filled with grace, for this kingdom is within you if you have it, (Luke 17:21), consisting in righteousness, peace, and joy in the Holy Spirit, (Rom. 14:17). Do you then bring all things to the King in subjection to his kingship? Every thought, every action, every whisper in the dark, into obedience? Do you concur with the rule of the Great King over

---

[44] "That at the name of Jesus every knee should bow, of things in heaven, and things in earth, and things under the earth; and that every tongue should confess that Jesus Christ is Lord, to the glory of God the Father," (Phil. 2:10-11).

[45] "...so that they are without excuse," (Rom. 1:20).

devils and the world, and the flesh? Do you give universal and sincere obedience, compliance, to the Great King now for the good of your soul?

How do you delight in praising him for his royalty? Have you ever done that? Psalm 145:1, "I will extoll thee, my God, O King." Is that your creed? It is the Christian's life ... to say with Thomas, "My Lord and My God." Psalm 47:6-7 says, "Sing praises to God, sing praises: sing praises to our king, sing praises: for God is the King of all the earth; sing ye praises with understanding." Does his Kingly rule and reign over you employ your tongues in such a way as to shout out his praises for who he is and what he has done with understanding? *Bellow them out with rejoicing* is the meaning there.

Think to yourselves, "It was for us sinners, that You, O Great King of generous love, went about doing good, preaching repentance, publishing the glad tidings of salvation of the kingdom, sending your disciples to preach the same, confirming your heavenly doctrine by many glorious miracles, and illustrating it by your Kingly power over the fall, for us sinners, that all our life would then be abundant life, as we touch the golden scepter held out to us as we approach your throne boldly, to see the attractive sweetness of love and pity to us who are not worthy, which, though, constrain us to praise and love you as the ruling and reigning King." Your creed, should be *Our God Reigns*, and so "may I with hearty repentance, boldly come to his throne for grace, bow in service before him." All this and more are what Jesus preached and meant when he said "repent, for the kingdom of heaven is at hand." And this we will consider more fully in his preached message in the next chapter.

Chapter 2: King Jesus and Kingdom Proclamation

"From that time Jesus began to preach, and to say, Repent: for the kingdom of heaven is at hand," (Matt. 4:17).

The *kingdom* is everywhere pronounced in Scripture as it is fulfilled in the coming of the Son of Man, the divine Christ.[1] God is the Great King, who is Kingly, has Kingship, and bestows this Kingship and Kingliness on his fellow, the Christ, who sits enthroned high and lofty and lifted up.

Jesus is the Messiah and the Eternal King who's dominion reigns over all absolutely, and over his church particularly. He preaches his kingdom, and in preaching it, preaches all the Scriptures summed up *in* the gospel, which is *our God reigns*; this God who is enthroned in heaven, and his kingdom has now come on you, so, *repent immediately*. God's kingship, (and all that it entails), and repentance, (and all that it entails), is the gospel message of the whole bible. It is the "what" of the gospel, and the Christ is the "how" of this gospel.

---

[1] 2 Sam. 7:12; Daniel 2:44, 4:34, 7:27; Micah 4:7; Psalm 145:13; Isa. 9:7; Luke 1:32; Acts 2:30, *etc.*

Remember, it is said of King Jesus that *his kingdom*, τῆς βασιλείας αὐτοῦ there will be no end (Luke 1:33), for the βασιλεία of Jesus Christ is also the βασιλεία of God.

Our God reigns through his Christ for his glory in his kingdom is the Gospel. Consider first, whose kingdom is it? It is the kingdom of God but received in a very special manner. In Christ's first sermon, he preaches this kingdom, and requires an *immediate* response, found in repentance, in order to receive his kingdom which *has come upon you*. Repentance from what? Repentance is in light of the fall of man and all the effects of the curse in breaking the Covenant of Works. In this fall, what happened that men need to repent? This comprises the Covenant of Works, in which Adam plunged all of humanity into the abyss of hell, unless the Great King intervenes over his subjects who are now in misery. Who will intervene? God intervenes. How does God do this? He does this through *King Jesus*. This anointed King is sent of the Father, in the power of the Spirit, to save his people from their sins, this is the substance of the *Old Testament* message. How is this saving to be done? Through the Mediator's work and merit, in substitutionary atonement, in which he rules and reigns over the fall for particular men and their redemption from the kingdom of darkness, of sin, death and the devil; this is the meaning of *Our God Reigns*, it is the meaning that the kingdom of heaven *is at hand.*

When Jesus says *repent*, he says this in light of the aforementioned points; in light of understanding the Old Testament Scriptures and their prophetic fulfillment in him.[2] Repentance is in light of the *kingly dominion* of the enthroned Christ, and of the fall that men are under. It is in light of the work of the Spirit in regeneration, in conversion, in a godly life according to the demands of King Jesus, in repentance because *Our God Reigns;* how will subjects in his kingdom act, and live, before him as a result? He desires to be beheld in all his kingly glory by everyone.

From all this, the concern of the βασιλεία as God's Kingly dominion, and Christ's proclamation of this, is saving (soteriological), so that any explanation of the kingdom stands or falls with the explanation of *covenantal salvation* in the preaching of the Christ, and in the preaching of his forerunner John the Baptist, as well as all his apostles preaching later on. The kingdom of God implies all of the preaching of Christ and his apostles explaining the covenant documents of the Old

---

[2] Old Testament sacrifices demonstrated *substitution* in the coming Messiah as a shadow of what would be fulfilled; this was seen in types and shadows. Christ fulfilled the temple rites being the High Priest of those called out of the world, and called to the Word of God. He merited, completed and fulfilled all Old Testament types and shadows so that the pure Gospel, the mystery of godliness, could be preserved and published in Spirit and truth, clearly and plainly.

Testament as they have been delivered to God's people. The whole of the New Testament message is εὐαγγέλιον, *good news*, that *God reigns over the fall*, and he does this ruling and reining from his high and lofty throne, *through his Christ* who sits upon that throne, for the glory of his name, by all his work and merit. Oftentimes, preachers will speak about the "how" of the gospel before they ever explain the "what or why" of the gospel. It is no wonder why so many do not understand the gospel, or that so few conversions are seen instantaneously, and rather occur, over long periods of time for many people in today's church. It is partly because in preaching the gospel, which is the means of conversion, preachers rarely explain the "who" of the gospel first, the "why" of the gospel second, and just jump to the "how" of the gospel third. Consider then, the preaching of both John the Baptist and Jesus. What did they preach?

What is the New Testament proclamation of the coming King in a fallen world? The concept of the kingdom was already present when John and Jesus proclaimed it to be near. This concept may be found in the Old Testament, in the LXX, and in Philo and Josephus, and apocalyptic literature of the day. The Jews were waiting for the King to come and deliver them from earthly tyrants. The *kingdom* is primarily God's kingly rule emerging in the dominant statement that, "it is near, or comes, or will come."[3] Men cannot

---

[3] Matt. 3:2; Mark 1:15; Luke 10:9-10; 21:31; 17:20; Matt. 12:28; Luke

arrogantly bring it in, but have to wait for it patiently, (1 Thess. 5:8, 19) like those who sow seed, (*cf.* Mark 4:26ff.), which is why the outwardly religious Jews that tried to have an outward religious system of seen religion, as the Pharisees, could not personally *usher* in the kingdom. It was not in their power to do so. The parables explain it as such; the parables of the mustard seed (Matt. 13:31–32), the leaven (Matt. 13:33), and the wheat and tares (Matt. 13:24ff.), the treasure and pearl (Matt. 13:44–45), the dragnet (Matt. 13:47ff.), the wicked servant (Matt. 18:23ff.), the laborers (Matt. 20:1ff.), the marriage feast (Matt. 22:2ff.), and the virgins (Matt. 25:1ff.); they are all *kingdom* parables, and often deal with *a tarrying time of patience*, never an *instant* earthly kingdom.

Christ was not the first to speak of the kingdom of God, and for that matter, nor was John the Baptist. The proclamation is set in the context that such a kingdom *already exists*. It existed before the human presence of either John as a preacher came on the scene, or God incarnate came preaching in the fullness of time. As looked at generally in the last chapter, it is an Old Testament concept, as is *every part* of the good news.

Both Christ and John proclaimed that the kingdom of God is *near*. There is no difference between the terms "kingdom of heaven" and "kingdom of God." Mark uses "kingdom of God" in 12:32 and 22:29.

11:20; 19:11; Matt. 6:10; 11:2.

Matthew uses it in 12:28; 19:24; 21:31, 43. But it was already *known* to those who heard them preach about it; no one was scratching their head thinking, "what is this new doctrine about some kind of kingdom?"

The kingdom being *upon a person*, "the kingdom of heaven is upon you", is principally the idea of God's dominion and rule breaking into the fallen world in order to exemplify his imperial majesty, power and right through the Messiah to reverse the fall in men, as it is particularly applied to their soul. Implied in the "who" and in the "what" is the "how." But without the *who* and the *what*, the *how* is more cryptically difficult to understand.[4] Implied in *God is king*, is designated, *Christ is the covenant Bearer who comes as the Suffering Servant to save his people from their sins.*[5] This was the substance of both John's preaching in announcing the coming of King Jesus, and in the preaching of Jesus announcing his coming as the Son of Man. This kingship and kingdom which John had in mind of the Christ, and Christ as the Son of Man now come, is opposed to everything temporal (earthly), to everything here and now, and requires an amendment of life to enter, while at the same time, it is a not yet "promise to come" in its fulfillment of all things in God's kingly reign. In the *future* there will be a *fulfilled kingdom* which the meek will inherit, and the righteous will finally enter. It is

---

[4] That means preaching the *how* without the *who* and *why* is going to make the Gospel more convoluted rather than clear.
[5] See Isaiah 53.

Chapter 2: King Jesus and Kingdom Proclamation

absolutely miraculous in every way. It is not just about what one gains from the kingdom that John and Jesus are concerned with. They are concerned with whether or not men *belong* to it or not, and whether the kingdom is actually *in them or not*. Men cannot usher in the kingdom into their heart, for the King must *bring them* into his kingdom, which is the theme of both the preaching of John and the Christ.

Christ and John the Baptist preached that God's divine kingship does not come merely with an "external show," but with supernatural repentance. A Pharisee was all about pointing to where *things that look like* God's kingdom might be. Maybe it was on the street corner where they prayed.[6] Maybe it was in the temple where they boasted.[7] Maybe it was within the tithing box where they put their tithe of mint and cumin.[8] No, no, the kingdom is *within man* and cannot be merely pointed out as hypocrites would make one think because it is not primarily of outward show, as it deals with its essence or foundation of the building first.[9] Both John and Jesus emphasize the negative fact that the Jew cannot make a mere claim to God's kingdom, as if they owned it, simply because they outwardly do things that look like *kingdom business*.[10] God breaks into the heart of

---

[6] Matthew 6:5.
[7] Luke 18:11.
[8] Matthew 23:23; Luke 11:42.
[9] "For other foundation can no man lay than that is laid, which is Jesus Christ," (1 Cor. 3:11).
[10] Matthew 3:9; Luke 3:8.

men with his kingdom, by the power of his Spirit, because of what the Christ has done.[11] There repentance is enacted, which is the central theme of amendment of life all through the Scriptures.[12] And as a result, the life of the one arrested by this reigning King will then be changed, and they will live their life in a manner in which shows themselves and others of this change; then and only then can the kingdom be seen.[13]

John cried out, "Repent ye: for the kingdom of heaven is at hand," (Matt. 3:2). "Then went out to him Jerusalem, and all Judaea, and all the region round about Jordan, and were baptized of him in Jordan, confessing their sins," (Matt. 3:5-6). Jesus preached the same, and in sending out his apostles, commanded they preach the same. "And as ye go, preach, saying, The kingdom of heaven is at hand," (Matt. 10:7). This is the gospel of the kingdom. Is it odd that the words are not, "Go and preach that I will die on a cross and then three days later be brought to life?" There is a reason for this, as we will see.

---

[11] "Not by works of righteousness which we have done, but according to his mercy he saved us, by the washing of regeneration, and renewing of the Holy Ghost," (Titus 3:5).
[12] Some examples are Jonah, after his punishment, (Jonah 2:2-9). The Ninevites, under the preaching of Jonah, (Jonah 3:5-9). The Jews, under the preaching of John the Baptist, (Matt. 3:6). The woman who anointed Jesus with oil, (Luke 7:37-48). The disobedient son, (Matt. 21:29). The prodigal son, (Luke 15:17-21). Peter after his denial of Jesus, (Matt. 26:75; Mark 14:72; Luke 22:62). The Ephesians, under the preaching of Paul, (Acts 19:18).
[13] "And be not conformed to this world: but be ye transformed by the renewing of your mind, that ye may prove what is that good, and acceptable, and perfect, will of God," (Rom. 12:2).

Who will receive the kingdom of God? Those who receive the kingdom are those who *repent*. Men receive it as the *gift* of God. God gives his kingdom: εὐδόκησεν ὁ πατὴρ ὑμῶν δοῦναι ὑμῖν τὴν βασιλείαν (Luke 12:32).[14] Jesus Christ promises the confessing Peter that he shall receive the keys of the kingdom: δώσω σοι τὰς κλεῖδας τῆς βασιλείας τῶν οὐρανῶν (Matt. 16:19). The kingdom is taken from the obstinate Jews and given to believers: ἀρθήσεται ἀφ' ὑμῶν ἡ βασιλεία τοῦ θεοῦ καὶ δοθήσεται ἔθνει ποιοῦντι τοὺς καρποὺς αὐτῆς (Matt. 21:43). And in this God calls Christians into his kingdom and glory: τοῦ θεοῦ τοῦ καλοῦντος ὑμᾶς εἰς τὴν ἑαυτοῦ βασιλείαν καὶ δόξαν (1 Thess. 2:12). God has set his people in the kingdom of the Son of his love: μετέστησεν εἰς τὴν βασιλείαν τοῦ υἱοῦ τῆς ἀγάπης αὐτοῦ (Col. 1:13). Believers are made worthy of the kingdom of God: καταξιωθῆναι ὑμᾶς τῆς βασιλείας τοῦ θεοῦ (2 Thess. 1:5). The Lord will deliver believers into his heavenly kingdom: ... ῥύσεταί με ὁ κύριος ... σώσει εἰς τὴν βασιλείαν αὐτοῦ τὴν ἐπουράνιον (2 Tim. 4:18). In this kingdom God makes promises to his people: ἐπηγγείλατο (James 2:5). The King has a divine right to close the kingdom to some men, but he opens it up as well: οὐαὶ ... ὅτι κλείετε τὴν βασιλείαν τῶν οὐρανῶν ἔμπροσθεν τῶν ἀνθρώπων (Matt. 23:13; *cf.* Luke 11:52).

---

[14] "Fear not, little flock; for it is your Father's good pleasure to give you the kingdom," (Luke 12:32).

What then do repentant believers do? They *receive* the kingdom. They receive the kingdom of God like a child: ὃς ἂν μὴ δέξηται τὴν βασιλείαν τοῦ θεοῦ ὡς παιδίον (Mark 10:15, Luke 18:17). They are distinguished by God to see the kingdom (to spiritually be enlightened to it), where others are hardened. Only the regenerate, the repentant, are worthy of this vision as Jesus taught Nicodemus. Christ taught him the Old Testament kingdom principle in John 3:3.[15] And what do they enter but, the kingdom: εἰσέρχεσθαι or εἰσπορεύεσθαι (*cf.* Matt. 5:20; 7:21; 18:3). The publicans and harlots will go into the kingdom before the self-righteous Pharisees: προάγουσιν ὑμᾶς εἰς τὴν βασιλείαν τοῦ θεοῦ (Matt. 21:31). The Jews should be υἱοὶ τῆς βασιλείας (Matt. 8:12) *sons of the kingdom*, but because of their hardness of heart they are not sons (*cf.* Matt. 13:38). Whosoever truly looks to King Jesus by repentance enters the kingdom, and they are able to enter the kingdom because the kingdom *first* enters them by the Spirit. Faith is required in this, for whatever is not of faith is sin (Rom. 14:23). Through *faith* men fight for the kingdom of God like the elect under the covenant in the Old Testament. "Who through faith subdued kingdoms, wrought righteousness, obtained promises," (Heb. 11:33). This

---

[15] "Jesus answered and said unto him, Verily, verily, I say unto thee, Except a man be born again, he cannot see the kingdom of God," (John 3:3). And then said to him, "Art thou a master of Israel, and knowest not these things?" (John 3:10).

kingdom bestowed of Christ belongs to the poor in spirit (Matt. 5:3), to those who are persecuted for righteousness' sake (Matt. 5:10); even to covenant children (Matt. 19:14). The kingdom is *eminently* covenantal. The invitation to the kingdom of God must be received in μετάνοια, *repentance*. For the sake of King Jesus, all the other "things" of this world, its riches and fame, must be abandoned, and men must look in repentance to the King. Men are not to be like those invited to the wedding who pleaded all kinds of obstacles (Matthew 22:1-14; Luke 14:16-24). For the sake of the kingdom of God, which is like the treasure hid in a field or the goodly pearl for which all else will be exchanged (Matt. 13:44-46), men must pluck out the eye or cut off the hand (Matt. 5:29ff). Anything that offends the King they are to throw away and cast off, and *then* enter in. What kind of faith is this, but *a radical faith?* It is a serious faith, to follow Christ's crown and covenant, for the kingdom of God requires the most serious decision, the most serious weeding out of the few from the many (Matt. 22:14). Spurious faith (unauthentic faith) is cultivated in the church by telling people, "just believe that Jesus saves you from your sins and all will be well." They will encourage people, "Write down the day of your salvation, on your "salvation card," put it in your wallet, and when you doubt your salvation because of your sinful life, just pull that card out, remind yourself what you did, and all will be well." But the King said, "No man, having put his hand to the plough, and looking back, is fit for the kingdom of God," (Luke 9:62). It is such a serious matter, to be kingdom children, that those who are invited by God to his kingdom and to his Christ must reflect on whether they can *really* receive the invitation with a whole heart, or not. Those who do so without realizing what it implies, or who hear without obeying, are like men building houses on sand (Matt. 7:24–27), and, "the fall thereof was great."

The King says, "not everyone who says to me, "Lord, Lord!" will enter into the kingdom of heaven, but those who do the will of my Father who is in heaven," (Matt. 7:21). Supreme readiness for service is demanded, even to the point of sacrifice of self, a denial of one's self,[16] a carrying of one's own cross, even of hatred of one's own family in comparison to Jesus (Matt. 10:37; Luke 14:26). What man left to himself is capable of answering that call of the Christ in such preaching? What man in his *own strength* can comply with the preaching of John the Baptist, or of the Christ, of Elijah or of Elisha, both typified in John and Jesus? Who thinks he can obey the Great King in this way? No one but Christ himself can follow God perfectly to serve God in all his glory. Men who try this without the Christ, are religious hypocrites.

---

[16] Matthew. 16:24, "Then said Jesus unto his disciples, If any man will come after me, let him deny himself, and take up his cross, and follow me." Luke 9:23, "And he said to them all, If any man will come after me, let him deny himself, and take up his cross daily, and follow me."

In this way, speaking of the kingdom, and of the preaching of the kingdom, one must speak about the Christ, the Mediator, the *how* of kingdom entrance.

Christ is the King and Deliverer. He is "king of the Jews," (Matt. 3:2; Mark 15:2). The people wanted him as king in a political sense; but he resists that in John 6:15. "When Jesus therefore perceived that they would come and take him by force, to make him a king, he departed again into a mountain himself alone." He is the promised "king of Israel" (Matt. 27:42; Mark 15:32), but they were looking for him to ride in on a white horse with an army, and not as a suffering Servant, to give his life a ransom for many; to die. He enters Jerusalem riding on a donkey as King, (Zech. 9:9; Matt. 21:5), and as such will conduct the last judgment as King, (Matt. 25:34). John even offers a Christological definition of the kingdom in John 18:37, "Pilate therefore said unto him, Art thou a king then? Jesus answered, Thou sayest that I am a king. To this end was I born, and for this cause came I into the world, that I should bear witness unto the truth. Every one that is of the truth heareth my voice." Such a Christ confesses his kingship, as it related to the truth of God. That he ... was born to be king as the God-man. ...was brought into the world to rule and reign. ...was sent for the cause of bearing witness to the truth of God's kingdom and covenant (1 John 5), testifies that all who love the truth, listen to him and hear *his voice*. He preaches he is King, and preaches that the kingdom is held out, and that men must honor his Kingship by repenting. In Revelation 19:16 John gives the royal title a cosmological dimension, where Christ is the King of *all kings*; find a king in any place, find a queen, or magistrate or president, and they are all subject to the King of heaven. Paul in 1 Tim. 6:16 says, "Which in his times he shall shew, who is the blessed and only Potentate, the King of kings, and Lord of lords," (1 Tim. 6:15). 1 Cor. 15:24 implies the kingship of Christ when it speaks of the subjection of all other rule, authority, and power until at last the kingdom is handed to the Father. Matthew describes Christ as "the great King" (Matthew 5:35), and the parables, are of the kingdom in which God exercises various *kingly* functions (Matt. 14:9; 18:23; 22:2, 7, 11, 13). In Christ's kingdom ... the angels will gather the evil ones and cast them out (Matt. 13:41), ... it will have no end (Luke 1:33), ... disciples will eat and drink in it (Luke 22:30), ... even the thief on the cross asks to be remembered when Christ comes into it in its fullness (Luke 23:42). It is not of this world (John 18:36). Entrance into this eternal kingdom is given to believing Christians (2 Peter 1:11). The mystery of the good news is that of the kingdom (Matt. 13:11). The Logos of God comes from and rules this kingdom (Matt. 13:19). The kingdom brings with it healings (Luke 9:2). The kingdom brings with it exorcisms against the forces of darkness (Matt. 12:28). Sinners have no inheritance in the kingdom of Christ and of God (Eph. 5:5). And ultimately, the kingdom of the world will become that of our Lord and his Christ (Rev. 11:15).

The kingdom of heaven is implied in the whole message of Christ and the apostles, for the kingdom is the gospel and the gospel is the kingdom, the rule and reign of King Jesus. As any of them explain it, the entirety of the kingdom in this is implied. It is the good news, the gospel of the kingdom (Mark 1:14; *cf.* Matt. 4:23; Luke 4:43; Acts 8:12), the gospel of the crucified One; the *how* of the *who, what* and *why*. When Paul says that, "I long to know nothing but Christ and him crucified,"[17] and other like sayings, he is preaching the *kingdom*, Christ, the King, the "who" and "what" of the kingdom, and his crucifixion, the mediatorial work of the Messiah in his kingdom work to save his people, the *how*; all that is the gospel. *Our God Reigns* through his Christ for his glory in his kingdom, and men can receive the benefits *if they repent*; this is Jesus' message, and the message of his apostles. If anyone desires to gain entrance, Jesus alone truly fulfils the demands of the kingdom, and they must look to him.

The kingdom of God is especially linked to the Anointed One. It is in Christ that the kingdom of David comes (Matt. 21:9; Mark 11:10). "For the kingdom's sake," in Luke 18:29 means "for my sake and the gospel's," in Mark 10:29, and, "for my name's sake," in

---

[17] "For I determined not to know any thing among you, save Jesus Christ, and him crucified," (1 Cor. 2:2). Compare, 1 Cor. 1:23 and Gal. 6:14.

Matt. 19:29. The kingdom of God in Mark 9:1 is the same as the Son of Man and his kingdom in Matt. 16:28. And Christ's kingdom is represented in the summary point of *repentance* in the coming and preaching of the Son of Man. Jesus Christ exceedingly endeavors the sinner's universal repentance and conversion in this, (Matt. 4:17; Mark 1:14-15; Luke 24:47; Acts 26:17-18). The dominion of God is manifest in the means and occasions of men's conversion. Some people, by some strong affliction, have had by divine sovereignty, their understandings awakened to consider conversion. Some have sat long under a preaching ministry and have been converted. Some have been converted in places that hardly have a trace of the gospel, but enough was there for them to be saved by the Spirit through the word (i.e. *regenerated*). The ordinary use of converting men to the kingdom is by *preaching*. "How then shall they call on him in whom they have not believed? and how shall they believe in him of whom they have not heard? and how shall they hear without a preacher?" (Rom. 10:14). Where is this phrase found on the lips of the prophet, priest and king of the Christ? *In his preaching.* If Christ is the sovereign King, all are to be obedient to his orders, for there they find the King of the kingdom working in their heart. Punishment necessarily follows on the doctrine of Christ's Kingly rule for those who do not obey, and this Son of Man, the divine King, will enact it readily and speedily at death, or his final coming.

Chapter 2: King Jesus and Kingdom Proclamation

Jesus' favorite designation of himself, is Son of Man, used some eighty times in the gospels. This is a *kingly* divine title from Daniel 7. It has nothing to do with being meek and lowly, but being kingly and powerful; it is attached to Daniel's understanding of the rule of the King, and preaching the kingdom (*cf.* Daniel 4 and 7).

The kingdom of heaven preached by Jesus is fulfilled by the "Son of Man" in the coming of the kingdom.[18] The "coming of the Son of Man," (Matt. 10:23) is synonymous with the, "coming of the kingdom of God," (Matthew 16:18 and Mark 9:1). "The Son of man shall send forth his angels, and they shall gather out of his kingdom all things that offend, and them which do iniquity," (Matt. 13:41). "...till they see the Son of Man coming in his kingdom," (Matt. 16:28). "That ye which have followed me, in the regeneration when the Son of man shall sit in the throne of his glory, ye also shall sit upon twelve thrones, judging the twelve tribes of Israel," (Matt. 19:28). "...when the Son of Man shall come in his glory" (Matt. 25:31), there, "the sitting of the Son of Man on the right hand of power and coming in the clouds of heaven" (Matt. 26:64). The divine God, the King, the Son of Man, is he who must accomplish all the obligations he has in the coming of the kingdom and to carry out the divine judgment, and in whose

---

[18] I have spent a great deal of time in the work *Seeing Christ Clearly* on the phrase "Son of Man," and you should look there to see that title more fully explained. But there are some things to note above.

hands, all authority has been placed, *and* who demonstrates the unsharable glory of God in his person. It is because the Son of Man is God. It is because the Son of Man is God the Great King. It is because the Son of Man is the perfect God-man who *takes away the sin of the world.* John the Baptist's conception of the kingdom not only implies repentance, but the coming King, who *is* the Son of Man, the Lamb who atones for sin; all these are one and the same Christ, and one and the same message.

The concepts "kingdom of heaven" and "Son of Man" proves that Jesus' preaching is concerned with the prophecy in Daniel 7:13ff. "I saw in the night visions, and, behold, one like the Son of man came with the clouds of heaven, and came to the Ancient of days, and they brought him near before him," (Daniel 7:13). In this prophecy, there the figure of the "Son of Man" as coming in the clouds of heaven to the "Ancient of Days," is he who is given dominion, and glory, and the kingship that was to comprise all the nations, and was to have an eternal and imperishable kingdom that never ends. Daniel 7 is an Old Testament prophecy and vision of Acts 1, where Christ ascends into heaven and surrounded by the glory cloud. In Daniel 7, Daniel sees the Christ as exalted, just after his ascension. Time is bent, so to speak, so that prophets in the Old Testament are given glimpses of events not accomplished yet in the New Testament. Though time seems to be linear to us, it's not. God is not bound by such time, and can give visions of the future to his prophets. This he does with Daniel. And this Son of Man is no ordinary man, and prophets of old are given glimpses of future truths about God's King and kingdom, and they know this. This is *no* ordinary man with earthly dominion. But in the Great Day of the Lord, he is the Divine Person who has unlimited divine authority, and to whom God's universal royal dominion has been entrusted. He sits on his Father's throne and rules the nations *with a rod of iron*. Jesus says in light of all this, "All power is given unto me in heaven and in earth," (Matt. 28:18). This, "Son of Man," is the Messiah. This Son of Man *is God.* This Son of Man is the King. This Son of Man reigns in his kingdom. And he says, then, "Repent, for the kingdom of heaven is at hand," that *Our God Reigns* through the *Christ* for his glory in his kingdom; so repent and do works worthy of repentance.

Is the kingdom of God within *you*? Is that a hard question for you to consider? It is the same as asking, do you believe the gospel? It is not in every man. Nor is the kingdom only a future thing, to come. The kingdom of God is *come unto you*, (Luke 11:20). The kingdom of God is come *upon you*, (Luke 10:9). The kingdom of God is *come nigh unto you* by the preaching of the gospel. ...by the coming and presence of the Messiah. And where is he, but as Scripture says, "but there standeth one *among* you," (John 1:26), for the Son of Man has come and brought in the rule of God. John the Baptist preached it as the forerunner, where Matthew 3:2 says, "The kingdom of heaven is at hand," and Christ went preaching *the gospel of the kingdom*, (Matt. 4:17, 11:12). If you hear the word of the kingdom, it is exclusive. It is not extended to every man in his heart, nor every hearer to their ears, but to those that hear the gospel, and receive it gladly ... those who hear the voice of the Shepherd. What a privilege it is to have heard it!

The kingdom is not a small gift. God holds out to you *a kingdom*. It is called *a kingdom*, because it offers men a *whole* kingdom, and all the *benefits* of a kingdom. There are far too many benefits even just to name, according to God's covenant. What shall we say about service to the Great King, for his crown and his covenant, set down with eternal life, abundant life, the gift of the Spirit, the renewing of a man, the imputation of Christ's righteousness, the way of peace, the fullness of the mystery of godliness, holiness, and all such benefits? It is no small gift indeed which required the life of the King to be laid down, and then to rise in glory and exaltation in his resurrection and ascension. What a privilege it is to have gained it if you have!

Labor to find that this kingdom of grace is truly in your heart. Heaven is God's throne, and the kingdom of heaven is within you if you are converted; and as God has said, "I will dwell in them, and walk in them, and they shall be my people, and I will be their God," (2 Cor. 6:16).

Chapter 2: King Jesus and Kingdom Proclamation

The seed of the kingdom was sown by Christ, and was reaped among the churches, and it was in them as a grain of mustard-seed, and in others it was as leaven hid in three measures of meal. And there the kingdom was preached, the gospel preached, and there were parables preached of the kingdom, and the world had it in the parables spoken to them. Those who believed John the Baptist's message came confessing their sins, and those who believe Jesus come confessing their sin, and penitent confessors all have this kingdom bestowed in sincerity in and on them, in the power of God to change them, to grant repentance through the work of Christ in his kingly dominion. *He that hath an ear, let him hear* what the power of the Spirit speaks, then shall be witnessed that which is written both of the power and of the kingdom. What a privilege it is to have found it!

This kingdom of God within us is our spiritual beauty. The kingdom of grace adorns you in the eyes of God and angels. This makes the king's daughter, the church, all glorious within. Grace sheds a glory and luster on the soul as it is changed into the Christ and follows his pattern and imitation. A heart beautified with grace has been worked on by the exertion and labor of the great King for your good. What a privilege it is to be transformed by it.

Such a kingdom of grace in the heart brings peace with it if you repent. Do not men desire peace of conscience, and peace of mind, and rest for their soul?

What peace moves in your heart and soul and mind for his glory? You were not at peace before you repented, and now you are at peace. If you have peace, Rom. 14:17, "The kingdom of God is ... righteousness, joy and peace in the Holy Ghost." Do you have this kingdom within you? Do you have this peace? Do you have the King's righteousness? Do you see its joyful effects? It is a peace which is bred out of his holiness. As the saying goes, "No holiness, no happiness." The coming of the Son of Man's kingdom is built on Kingly holiness, which is *repentance* for fallen people who need to be changed. The kingdom of grace is a kingdom of peace with God. But it is a kingdom of non-negotiable action in continual repenting. "Wherefore I abhor myself, and repent in dust and ashes," (Job 42:6).

Such a kingdom improves and develops the soul for the glory of the Great King. Believers are to be rich in grace (James 3:5). "Shall he not give us all things?" Thomas Watson said, "A man may be rich in bills and bonds; a believer, though, he may say as Peter, "Silver and gold have I none, (Acts 3:6), yet he is rich in bills and bonds, he is heir to all God's promises; and to be heir to the promises, is better than to be heir to the crown of England."[19] Such a kingdom establishes this peace, and established a friendship with God. "My heart is fixed, O God, my heart is fixed: I will sing and give praise," (Psa. 57:7), without which, the heart is

---

[19] Watson, Thomas, *A Body of Practical Divinity*, (Carlisle, PA: The Banner of Truth Trust, 1990) 110.

anxious and worrisome. This kingdom of grace is distinguishing in this way. It is a sure pledge of God's love, but upon the condition of repentance. God may give kingdoms in anger, but wherever the kingdom of grace is set up, it is in love. God cannot give grace in anger; how could that be? The crown always goes with this kingdom to his people. Let us be determined to gain much from this kingdom of grace. And when we find much, we too will cast our crowns at his feet to exalt his glory and not our own. What a privilege it is to be beautified by it!

What kind of comfort will you glean from this kingdom brought in by the Son of Man? In his dominion and universal Kingship, the Son of Man brings peace, grace and holiness for you. He brings love to his people which is as great as his Kingly dominion. And though the Son of Man as Isaiah said, is high and lofty and lifted up, and though he sits enthroned majestically in the heavens as the great king, and though he ushers in a kingdom of universal and absolute rule over the fall, yet it is a throne, "encircled with a rainbow," as Ezekiel 1:28 says, showing that he loves his people in the Christ in his covenant. He even presses them to come boldly to this throne, to find more and more peace, and more and more grace, and presses them to ask, Isa. 45:11, "Ask of me things to come concerning my sons, and concerning the work of my hands command you me." As if he were to say, "plead with me the promises of my kingdom, and you will find me as willing to perform my word, and gratify your desires, as if "I were rather under your authority, than you under mine," as Stephen Charnock said.[20] This is as if God would say to you, "My word stands, and my dominion stands, so plead my promises in prayer and you shall have them as if you command me, for my golden scepter is held out to you, and you may approach and command what you will as it is my will." He rules as a Father, by love to you as well as by authority. He holds out his golden scepter and extends it to the sons and daughters of his kingdom, by his Christ. Plead his will and you will have it. What a privilege it is to reap comfort by it.

All earthly kingdoms will come to nothing, but the kingdom of God within you, shall remain as Mount Zion. It shall never be shaken. Never, then forget the place of your peace, and the place of your grace in King Jesus, who will come and lead you with his sweet spices, and the savor of his ointment.

Do not think, like hypocrites do, that you can expect a bed of rest in the barren wilderness of your own performances and righteousness, since God has appointed a spiritual kingdom to be your rest now. And in the midst of sin and misery, the fall-reversing power of the Christ will attend you in your walk, so pray in faith, without wavering, that the Lord Jesus would by

---

[20] Charnock, Stephen, *The Works of Stephen Charnock*, Volume 2 (London: Printed for Ben. Griffen and Thomas Cockeril, 1684). Reprinted., ed. T. Smith, intro, by James M'Cosh. (Edinburgh: James Nichol, 1864-66) 481.

his Spirit lead you to that Rock which is infinitely higher then yourself, and fix your eye of faith on that brazen Serpent the Lord Jesus who is made to us of God, wisdom, righteousness, sanctification and redemption by his Kingly work; high and lifted up. One vision of him will press you to defy to the worst temptation and lust as nothing, and one look to the Son of Man will overcome all the powers of darkness combined, that you might bear the marks of his kingdom. In the King, you can be *more* than conquerors; not merely conquerors, *more than conquerors*. Here you can be conquering all spiritual wickedness in heavenly places, and in your heart, for you can do all things in Christ who strengthens you.

Your soul must be quieted and established on the King, and in submission set under his Kingly reign. He is filled with soul-astonishing riches of grace, so make your boast of him to God for what you need and what you desire. Christ is the King who will lead us forth with perfect boldness, not only to look in the face of, but to trample on the most terrible of our adversaries, sin, our own righteousness, death, Satan, and hell itself, through the great and glorious conquest of our Captain and King. He has led captivity captive, in whom God always beholds us, and in whose righteousness, we shall be found, being not only delivered from this present evil world, but made freely ready to be partakers of the inheritance of the saints in light in his kingdom.

The Kingdom of Heaven is Upon You

Surely the bright and glorious appearance of God in you, and the high Spirit of faith and prayer, is set and fixed in the condition of kingdom reception which is godly repentance, and faith in Christ. I have written about repentance so many times in the past,[21] but yet, in repentance, you must think, "The kingdom of heaven is within me. It is in my soul, and I can now, and do, by his power in me, all things. I can do more than some things. I can govern and command all my inward and outward senses, that all the affections and powers of the old man in my soul are conquered, and are in subjection to the new man in me by that godly repentance which God has bestowed on me by his Son day by day. And this kingdom, which now rules and reigns in my heart is the greatest kingdom of all, better than all earthly kingdoms, scepters, crowns and glories that this world could ever offer. All these promises to me, have their beginning in this life, and perfected in the life to come. My King tells me that his kingdom of heaven is within me. And this I will believe all the days of my life, and make my profession answerable to my life, answerable to the King." This is to live a life of mourning, poverty of spirit, of repentance. What a privilege it is to have it bestowed in full on you!

If you do not find the kingdom of God and the kingdom of heaven within you, in this world, be assured you will not ever find it in the world to come

---

[21] See my work *Joseph's Resolve and the Unreasonableness of Sinning Against God*.

within you, but enacted upon you. "He that denies me before men, him will I deny before my Father which is in Heaven." The soul that does not enjoy the King and his kingdom now, he shall never enjoy it after. How shall you take hold of the kingdom if you don't have it, or that your grasp on it seems to be slipping? Scripture teaches that sinners repenting of their sins, and turn from them to God, which encourages you to *imitate them* in this narrow way of finding life and salvation; for Jesus says, *few there be that find it.*

I will give you some, by way of mention. Manasseh, (2 Chron. 33:12-18). John the Baptist's hearers, (Matt. 3:2, 5-8). The sinful woman, (Luke 7:37). Zachaeus the Publican, (Luke 19:7-10). The prodigal son, (Luke 15:15ff). Saul the persecutor, (Acts 9:3-23). Lydia, (Acts 16:14-15). The jailor and his house, (Acts 16:25-35). Many Gentiles, (Acts 11:18 and 15:19). Many at Ephesus, (Acts 19:17-21). The Thessalonians, (1 Thess. 1:5-11). The thief on the cross, (Luke 23:40-44). They that crucified, and consented to the death of the Lord Jesus Christ, even 3000 of them saved, (Acts 2:36-37). All these are examples to press you to take hold of *repentance* that is held out by Christ in giving you a kingdom.

To reject King Jesus is to be impenitent; it is the opposite of what Christ preached. It is rebellion against God's command; opposite to his kingdom. God will not clear the impenitent; they are guilty of not heeding his laws and listening to his words of truth. And how terrible is that state of sin and misery if one dies in that state! He is eternally shut out of God's kingdom, (Matt. 18:3, 5). He treasures up wrath against the day of wrath, (Rom. 2:5-6). God renders their condition who live under the gospel, worse than that of heathens at the Judgement, (Matt. 11:20-25). And it exposes impenitent people to all the judgements of the Son of Man both in this present world and in the world to come, (Luke 13:3-5; Ezek. 18:20, 26, 30-31). How terrible!

    Divine repentance removes the natural man's sinfulness, no matter how great it might be, (Isa. 1:16-18 and 55:7). By repentance a sinner, out of the sight and sense, not only of the danger, but also of the filthiness of his sins, as contrary to the holy nature and righteous law of the King, and on the understanding the kingdom is held out in mercy in Christ, grieves for and hates his sins as to turn from them all to the King, purposing and endeavoring to walk with him in all the ways of his commandments.[22] It doesn't matter how deep sin is or how wide it has stretched, Christ the King is able to pardon it; for he is greater than you are, and a greater Savior than you are a sinner, and his golden scepter is extended to all who desire to touch of it. Such a repentance is the way to life and salvation, (Acts 11:18; 2 Cor. 7:10), by Christ's way, the only way, the highway of holiness, by that supernatural change of mind. And such a work in your soul by the Spirit will put you into possession of the inheritance of the saints, of the

---

[22] This is the *1647 Westminster Confession of Faith* 15:2.

kingdom of heaven, Paradise, and of King Jesus himself (Acts 26:18; Matt. 18:3; Luke 23:41-43). All this, and more, that I have said here, is encapsulated in the words of the Christ, "repent, for the kingdom of heaven is at hand." And in the next chapter we will consider *the kingdom ushered in.*

Chapter 3:
King Jesus' Requirement for Entry into His Kingdom

"From that time Jesus began to preach, and to say, Repent: for the kingdom of heaven is at hand," (Matt. 4:17).

As a reminder, the *kingdom* is everywhere pronounced as it is fulfilled in the coming of the Son of Man, the divine Christ. God is King, who is Kingly, has Kingship, and bestows this Kingship and Kingliness on his fellow, the Christ, who sits enthroned high and lofty and lifted up. Jesus is the Messiah and the King who's dominion reigns over all. He preaches his kingdom, and in preaching it, preaches all the Scripture summed up in the gospel, which is *Our God Reigns*, who is enthroned in heaven, and the kingdom of this God *has come upon you*, so *repent*. God's kingship, and all that it entails, and repentance, and all that it entails is the gospel message of the whole bible. It is the what of the gospel, and the Christ is the how of the gospel. It is said of King Jesus τῆς βασιλείας αὐτοῦ there will be no end (Luke 1:33). For the βασιλεία of Jesus Christ is also the βασιλεία of God. But, how does one get into this kingdom that Jesus preached about?

Repentance is required to enter into the kingdom of heaven. The kingdom of God announced by

Chapter 3: King Jesus' Requirement for Kingdom Entry

Christ is entirely from the view of God's divine kingship. This coming of the kingdom is preeminently the idea of God's dominion and kingly self-assertion, of his coming to the world in order to reveal his royal majesty, power and right over the world and over the fall, for his glory. This is the basic premise of all Christ's preaching. It is a particular message of *dominion, redemption* and of *judgment* according to the *character* of the King. The kingdom means *dominion and redemption*, because God maintains his royal justice towards those who put their trust in him as his people, and see they are under his authority.[1] And it means *judgment* because God maintains his royal will in opposition to all who resist his will. Israel is called to repent, and the nations of the world are called to repent. In light of the great coming King, the first condition and obligation of sinners is conversion, transformation and alteration; and that universally and immediately. The Pharisees cannot make an appeal to being Abraham's children; there is no change there.[2] Anyone who desires to flee from the wrath to come, this divine judgment brought forth by the King of the universe, must bring forth fruits *worthy* of repentance; this means it must be true repentance, not fake. And nothing and no one will oppose his Kingship in this way. No one should ever be

---

[1] "I am the LORD thy God, which have brought thee out of the land of Egypt, out of the house of bondage," (Exod. 20:2).

[2] "They answered and said unto him, Abraham is our father. Jesus saith unto them, If ye were Abraham's children, ye would do the works of Abraham," (John 8:39).

content with a *general repentance*, but it is every man's duty to endeavor to repent of his precise sins *particularly*, and every man is bound to make private confession of his sins to God, praying for their pardon, on which, and by forsaking them, he shall find mercy. This view is what Jesus preached, and it was his gospel.

"I object!" one might say and press, "The gospel is *Christ crucified*, which Paul longed to know, knowing *nothing* but that." When Jesus preached, he began at the *who*, *what* and *why*, not the *how*; that should cause all good preachers to pause about how to preach the kingdom and the gospel. But what is Jesus' preaching? We will see in the next chapter that it is *certainly* the work of the Mediator. But this is not how Christ *begins* his preaching. "Now after that John was put in prison, Jesus came into Galilee, *preaching the gospel of the kingdom of God*, and saying, [What did he say?] The time is fulfilled, and the kingdom of God is at hand: repent ye, and believe the gospel," (Mark 1:14-15). And what is the gospel of the kingdom? Christ preached the commission given to him of the Father, to publish the good news of God's kingdom and rule, the good tiding that *Our God Reigns*, its construction and success by the Son of Man, and likewise to declare its nature, and the method of admittance into it, which is *repentance*. When a soul is under the inward kingdom and government of the Christ, the Lord with all his royalty, in and by the gospel of pure grace, the golden scepter of Christ's kingdom and Christ himself is received. The kingdom of God has then come to that soul, and entered into that heart, and so the gospel, the good news, is that fallen men have received the gospel of the kingdom. "Believe and repent, for the kingdom of God is at hand." And under this understanding much is set down according to the Scriptures, but King Jesus is ready to enter the souls of his people. God has seized the government of the world for his purpose to make himself known. Christ is ascended as the high and lofty one on his throne as the Redeemer with glory and power. He reigns! So, the *good news* of these swift-footed messengers who preach the gospel of peace, demonstrate the gospel of the kingdom of God is at hand, and it must be proclaimed *for God, about God, and to the glory of God*. The kingdom of God and the gospel are the same, and entry to God's kingdom is *repenting*.

As it concerns the Christian's daily prayers, the petition for the coming of the kingdom is placed between the one hallowing of God's name (which is a petition and ought to be a daily prayer for holiness) and the one for the obedience to his will, "thy will be done," (Matt. 6:9-10). Men must, 1) hallow God's name, and, 2) carry out the will of the King. In this is the coming and expansion of the kingdom in arresting this world; this is what Christ even *tells his disciples to pray for in the Lord's Prayer*.[3]

---

[3] "Thy kingdom come," (Matt. 6:10). If the Bridegroom tarries, we pray, annexed to this, that the kingdom would come in its

The Christ has come to call, "sinners to repentance" (Mark 2:17ff), that they may be translated out of the dominion of darkness into the kingdom of God's beloved Son;[4] Jesus has not come to destroy the law or the prophets, all God's holy will, in which love to God and to one's neighbor is found, on which hang the whole bible, but, "to fulfill them," (Matt. 5:17). He comes, "to proclaim the kingdom of God," (Mark 1:38), the good tidings of the gospel. That God is King, but the King is Immanuel, God with us *incarnate*.[5] Which is why he was sent of the Father to do such, "I have been sent," (cf. Matt. 10:40). The Son of Man has come, "to seek and to save that which was lost," (Luke 19:10); to minister, and to give his life a ransom for many, (Mark 10:45; Matt. 20:28; *cf*. also Matt. 11:18-19; Luke 7:33-34). In God's Kingly dominion, there is now hope for sinners, in that God rules and reigns over the *misery* of the fall, and can reverse its affects, in fact, make whole new men of old dead corpses through his Son; that is how powerful his Spirit is in this kingdom. He does this by the power and authority of the Christ, who is the enthroned King, in and by his covenant.

Repentance is a requirement to enter Christ's covenantal kingdom. When man was first created by

---

expansion over the whole world, the church, and in our own minds and hearts.

[4] "Who hath delivered us from the power of darkness, and hath translated us into the kingdom of his dear Son," (Col. 1:13).

[5] See my work *God For Us* for a larger discussion of the incarnation in this way.

God, he was happy in righteousness, holiness and divine knowledge. As long as he kept that covenant of life, he kept the state of his nature, and so he continued in that righteous way. He enjoyed his Maker's favor, he walked with God, had a friendly relationship with him. In this he continually made a thankful acknowledgment of his dependence upon God's kingly dominion and instruction, as he saw God's goodness, and performed due obedience to his divine will. In this he was set under God's providence and with great happiness, dwelling in the Paradise of Eden, the Garden of God's delight.

Through the breach of the covenant, man fell from his happiness.[6] He was not content with what God had done for him, and wanted to provide a better way for himself. So disregarding God's kingly dominion, he cast himself out of God's kingly favor, and with himself, his posterity, treading in the same steps of disobedience, they now are cursed with a miserable inheritance which he left them. The unhappiness of this estate was so heavy, it cast them all headlong into the curse of eternal death and hell.

However, the merciful King, the Son of Man, the Son of God, with an unspeakable compassion, interfered between them and the dreadful eternal ruin of God's kingly wrath. He interceded for their pardon.

---

[6] "...and they have broken my covenant," (Ezek. 44:7). "But they like *men* have transgressed the covenant: there have they dealt treacherously against me," (Hosea 6:7). *Men* is translated as אָדָם 'adam. They, like Adam, have transgressed the covenant.

He broke in to save them when they did not cry out, nor even look for him, but rather hated him.

    The eternal Father was highly pleased with Christ's mediation;[7] and for his sake he did not lock the door of hope against the first rebellious sinner who scoffed at his laws in that Garden Paradise, and neither did he afterward shut up his disobedient children in the irrecoverable wretchedness of their sin and rebellion. He did not leave them in the field of blood to wallow in their own misery there.[8] Though they cast themselves out of the mercies of the ancient covenant, by breaking its conditions, yet the Son of God was pleased to be the messenger of a New Covenant, and brought this message in its fullness from heaven. Even at the original sin itself, there is seen the good news of that reigning and ruling God over sin where he would send a mediator, one to crush the serpent's head. In Genesis 3:15 God says, "I will put...enmity..." what a very interesting phrase *that* is. God does this; he puts enmity between the woman and the devil. But, the Son of Man will come and crush the head of the serpentine deceiver; that old dragon.[9]

---

[7] "Thou art my beloved Son; in thee I am well pleased," (Luke 3:22).
[8] Ezekiel 16:6, 8.
[9] Revelation 12:9, "And the great dragon was cast out, that old serpent, called the Devil, and Satan, which deceiveth the whole world: he was cast out into the earth, and his angels were cast out with him." Revelation 20:2, "And he laid hold on the dragon, that old serpent, which is the Devil, and Satan, and bound him a thousand years."

When this incarnate God-man came into the world at the time of fulfillment, God sent his celestial messengers at his birth to proclaim the good-will which was contained in this kingly dominion.[10] The Christ sealed this message and work with his blood, which when he was going to die, he said he would shed for the remission of sins.[11] And having performed that promise full of unspeakable kindness and glorious benefits, when he was raised from the dead, he commanded his servants, whom he had given and ordained to the ministry of the good news of the kingdom, the sure design of his mercy, that they should publish it to all the world, and in his name preach ...what? They were to preach the *kingdom of God in repentance*, and on *that* promise, forgiveness of sin.[12] They were to declare that God would now accept the sinner's return to the duty and service of worship to the Father by grace, through faith in Christ; but *not without*

---

[10] "Glory to God in the highest, and on earth peace, good will toward men," (Luke 2:14).
[11] "Whom God hath set forth to be a propitiation through faith in his blood, to declare his righteousness for the remission of sins that are past, through the forbearance of God," (Rom. 3:25).
[12] "And as ye go, preach, saying, The kingdom of heaven is at hand," (Matt. 10:7). "And this gospel of the kingdom shall be preached in all the world for a witness unto all nations; and then shall the end come," (Matt. 24:14). "And he sent them to preach the kingdom of God, and to heal the sick," (Luke 9:2). "The law and the prophets were until John: since that time the kingdom of God is preached, and every man presseth into it," (Luke 16:16). "Preaching the kingdom of God, and teaching those things which concern the Lord Jesus Christ, with all confidence, no man forbidding him," (Acts 28:31).

turning. And that anyone of all sinful mankind could escape that disobedient and rebellious state, by the work necessary to receive the kingdom, by acknowledging their sins, mourn their rebellion, throw down their arms being at war with God as wicked rebels, yield to mercy, and return to their allegiance to the High King ... if they repent. In this they could gain, by God's allowance, the way of happiness again. For by the forgiveness of their sins God restores them to his favor, and they can obtain peace, and receive a new kingdom in them. This entrance into the celestial kingdom is by way of godly repentance. *Repentance* is a change of mind as to what is past, and it carries in it a better care for what is future in the service of the great King. It comprises sight of sin, sorrow for sin, confession of sin, shame for sin, hatred of sin and turning from sin, all which are an evangelical graces given by the Spirit of God because of the work of King Jesus.[13]

    Repentance is a *supernatural* grace. Repentance is a grace given and bestowed by God's Spirit.[14] Are there saving merits, or steps to salvation, found in the light of nature? None whatsoever. If men seek salvation,

---

[13] 1647 *Westminster Larger Catechism*, Question 76. "Repentance unto life is an evangelical grace." It teaches this thought more thoroughly where it asks the question, "What is repentance unto life?" It answers, "Repentance unto life is a saving grace, wrought in the heart of a sinner by the Spirit and word of God."(2 Timothy 2:25; Zechariah 12:10).

[14] "...if *God* peradventure will give them repentance to the acknowledging of the truth," (2 Tim. 2:25).

life, and the immortality of the heavenly kingdom, then there is no other to whom they may flee, seeing that God alone is the fountain of life, the anchor of salvation, and heir of the kingdom of heaven. All those whom God has adopted as his sons are said to have been chosen not in themselves but in his Christ (Ephesians 1:4), not of the will of the flesh nor of man but of God (John 1:13), and this truth is found in God's word alone (Psalm 19:7). For unless God could love them in Christ, he could not honor them with the inheritance of his kingdom if they had not previously become partakers of him; how will God honor rebels? He curses and judges rebels in their sin. He does not *honor* them. But in Christ, the eternal Word, then, is the mirror in which men must, and without self-deception, contemplate their own election in grace.[15] In the Beloved; in him, by him alone. The blessings of the Spirit of God are only given to men when they are regenerated. They do not obtain any measure of grace unless they are regenerated and have been given repentance and saving faith.[16] Regeneration does not come through natural revelation but by the sovereign operation of the Spirit on the heart, soul and mind. Grace is not common, but particular. Repentance and

---

[15] Keep in mind people are not instructed to *prove out their election*. Rather, they are to make their calling and election sure by looking at the fruit of repentance in their life. They demonstrate their faith, prove that out, and then never doubt of their election.
[16] "For by grace are ye saved through faith; and that not of yourselves: it is the gift of God," (Eph. 2:8).

faith in this are a singular gift of God to them. The counterfeit repentance of ones who are like *Esau* and *Judas* are rejected; it does no good being carnal.[17] Believing sinners, one who is sensibly and discernably affected with and afflicted for his sin as committed against God, freely confesses, and fervently pleads for pardon, turns from all sin to the only Savior, King Jesus. But even before they can do this, being *born again* by the Spirit precedes repentance, or repentance will be like that of Esau, tears without change.[18] Esau sought the blessing with tears, doing more than what most Christians will do; how many Christians will cry over sin today? Repentance is supernatural, and part of the renewed ability of the believer because the Spirit has worked on their soul.

Repentance precedes God's pardon. Justification does not come before repentance. Men must turn and repent, and then they are *declared just* in the sight of God by believing in Jesus Christ alone for salvation by faith. Repentance houses in it, a turning from sin to God. Oh, that most difficult word, *turning*. It is not merely confession, or shame, or sorrow, or even hatred of sin, of all sin, but the ending of that supernatural work, that *turning* from it, is so hard! If one *does not turn* from sin, have they really done what is

---

[17] "Because the carnal mind is enmity against God: for it is not subject to the law of God, neither indeed can be," (Rom. 8:7).
[18] "...he was rejected: for he found no place of repentance, though he sought it carefully with tears," (Heb. 12:17).

Chapter 3: King Jesus' Requirement for Kingdom Entry

necessary to receive the kingdom when they are converted? Jesus requires immediate and universal repentance. He requires new men, not halfhearted men, or partial reform.[19] The very word *repentance* is a *change of mind*, a *universal* change. There is no room for repentance in a person's life if they don't see their sin.[20] People today often reject what occurred in the covenant in the garden. They will not have themselves represented by another in sin and for someone else to *ruin them*. They don't like it that God considers them *evil* as a result of what *Adam* did. But because of the fall, *Jesus calls people evil*. "If ye then, being evil..." (Matt. 7:11). God requires everyone to be *perfect*. Jesus Christ in that same sermon said, "Be ye therefore perfect, even as your Father which is in heaven is perfect, (Matt. 5:48). Perfect? Yes, God requires perfection. And if they are not perfect, the King requires universal repentance from a changed heart.

Imperfect people, according to God's law, are evil because they are imperfect sinners who are cursed with original sin, and they disobey God's word.[21] The soul that perceives it is evil before God, knows its fate is an eternal punishment in hell for his original sin nature and inclination to further sin.[22] He knows all he

---

[19] "Ephraim is a cake not turned," (Hosea 7:8).
[20] "I came not to call the righteous, but sinners to repentance," (Luke 5:32).
[21] "If ye then, being evil, know how to give good gifts unto your children, how much more shall your Father which is in heaven give good things to them that ask him?" (Matt. 7:11).

does aggravates such a terrible state, but if he turns to God, fully, not partially, not in halves, not in some things, but in all things, that he is afflicted for the guilt of his sin, he not only sees that he is a true sinner before God, but sorrows under his understanding of sin, and is ashamed of such a sad and sinful state. He comes to learn that repentance is a supernatural gift given to him *from* God, and that he must turn from sin and confess his sin by the power of the Spirit. This is not an option for receiving the kingdom, it is *necessary*, the condition by which he may receive it, for *Jesus required universal and immediate repentance in his preaching to those that desired his kingdom.* True and full repentance is necessary to remove the wrath and judgments of God, and to, "answer the call of the gospel," which requires *everyone* to repent. King Jesus, "now commandeth all men every where to repent," (Acts 17:30).

In the characteristics of true biblical repentance people must contemplate whether or not they have a counterfeit repentance which emulates Esau, Judas and Saul, or a biblical repentance that emulates Moses, David and the Apostle Paul. Repentance is God's gift, "if God peradventure *will give them* repentance to the acknowledging of the truth," (2 Tim. 2:25). "Then hath God also to the Gentiles *granted* repentance unto life," (Acts 11:18). None of the means of grace are effectual without God's blessing and Spirit in them. *God* gives

---

[22] "...the face of the Lord is against them that do evil," (1 Peter 3:12).

repentance, and people must pursue the supernatural grace of repentance, without which, they cannot receive his kingdom.

Repentant sinners are awakened with certain impressions of the Spirit to know their sinfulness, and that this sin nature must be reckoned by God's holy standards.[23] When such people feel and groan under the pain and burden of their sin, they are made sensible by the Spirit to God's holy word. Sight of sin will press men to consider the torture of the second death; which he knows is justifiably certain.

Jesus in proclaiming the kingdom, requiring repentance, is really requiring true biblical reformation. Such is always a thorough reform, not a partial one. That is why individuals can never have "sort of" repentance, or "sort of" a reformation. I remember leading a fellow to repent of his sin. He prayed that God would forgive him. He prayed that Christ would save him. He prayed that he would be pardoned. After the prayer he was giddy, manifestly so, outwardly, as if a change took place, seen in his countenance and face. Then I said, "now ... you have to be holy. You have to give up fornication," knowing that he was of that kind of person. This fellow was saddened in this, immediately. He confessed his sin and knew he needed the King to grant him pardon, but when he was pressed to hate *all* his sin, and *turn* from it, he rejected that, and walked out. And on his walking out, he said, "I will not

---

[23] "The eyes of your understanding being enlightened," (Eph. 1:18).

give that up." He was no longer giddy but *angry* with the King to require him to obey him; he did not like the gospel of the kingdom, but he would have gladly taken free grace, or *the crown without the cross*. How many churches are filled up with such people today? The doctrine of repentance is not, as many suppose, *just confession of sin*. No. Can a man say, "Lord, I want to have a life of blessing, without holiness? I am only going to take care of some things in my life, but not all things. I am not resolved to take care of it all, but only some of it," and think the King will grant his pardon. Will God give such hypocrites a kingdom?

Repentance is not a bare, single, and transient action,[24] as ignorant souls imagine. The repentance which is given of God, is not a fleshly action, but power, principle, and frame of spirit that is given by the Spirit of power to overcome sin in reversing the fall, *it makes dead men new men*. The power and principle are divine, but the act and exercise of repentance is by men, and that continually in this life. God will grant supernatural repentance to men, but not without men. God will not save men without men. He never saves men without them, for they must repent and believe him. He requires *their* repentance. God plants the root by which man brings forth fruit worthy of repentance,

---

[24] For a full discussion of this, see this eBook work by Zachary Crofton (1626-1672), *The Nature, Necessity and Character of True Repentance*, (Crossville, TN: Puritan Publications, 2016) section on *The Nature of True Repentance* in Chapter 1.

(Matt. 3:8). "And I will pour upon the house of David, and upon the inhabitants of Jerusalem, the spirit of grace and of supplications: and they shall look upon me whom they have pierced, and they shall mourn for him, as one mourneth for his only son, and shall be in bitterness for him, as one that is in bitterness for his firstborn," (Zech. 12:10-11). Look at some of these ideas from Zechariah, grace, mourning, bitterness, and such divine works. Repentance is not the work of an hour, or a day, but a constant frame, course and bent of the soul. To receive Christ's kingdom, and to continue to receive it, is a divine and supernatural act of faith, yet, housed in repentance. A turning from sin (*repentance*) and a turning to Christ (*by faith*). It begins, and then brings forth renewed acts, and that *always*.[25]

It is a grace freely given from above; not acquired by any means or merit of men. It springs into the soul by the good-will of God, and power of the Holy Spirit. "Good and perfect gift[s], [are] from above, and cometh down from the Father of lights," (James 1:17). Only King Jesus, by way of his covenant, can, "take away the stony heart, and give a heart of flesh," (Ezek. 36:26). It is the sole and singular prerogative of Christ the King exalted, "to give repentance." Zachary Crofton said, "Repentance is not the result of a pure nature, nor yet the effect of the law; but a pure gospel-grace; preached by the gospel, promised in the

---

[25] "For godly sorrow worketh repentance to salvation not to be repented of," (2 Cor. 7:10).

covenant, sealed in baptism, produced by the Spirit, properly flowing from the blood of Christ; and so is every way supernatural; so that every returning sinner must pray to God. "Turn thou me, and I shall be turned;" (Jer. 31:18-19), and the praise of repentance obtained must be returned to God alone, as coming from him whom it has been derived, (1 Peter 1:3); for it is a supernatural grace."[26]

The believing sinner is the *subject* of repentance. The soul in this, spreads before itself the law of God. It surveys the past course of his own life. It sentences himself as accursed of God, and bound over to Divine fury. But the soul is not only acquainted with, but afflicted for its guilt; it not only sees that it is a sinner, but sorrows under, and is ashamed of such a sad and sinful state.

God ordains this method of giving repentance for various wise and gracious ends. To suit them for, and engage them to set an esteem on Christ Jesus, and the remission of sin through him alone. To set them at enmity with sin, and in due submission to his sacred Kingly will. It must be, though, a turning from all sin to God. This is the formality of true repentance. There must be a rejection of sin, and a return to the King's highway.[27] This must spring from conviction, and spread itself into condemnation. Shame and sorrow

---

[26] Crofton, *Ibid*.
[27] "And an highway shall be there, and a way, and it shall be called *the way of holiness*," (Isa. 35:8).

must seize on the confessing sinner. How will one *hate and turn* without *shame and sorrow* in sin's *sight* towards a godly confession?

To receive the kingdom of Christ one *must* repent. It is, in point of fact, a privilege of the gospel of the kingdom to do so. It is a change of mind as to what is past. A person who repents must begin with a condemnation of his former life. How can a man repent of what he has done, who does not condemn it as wicked? This part of repentance expresses itself in two points: 1. humble confession of sin, and, 2. earnest prayer for pardon.

Humble confession of sin, is required to receive the kingdom.[28] The one that truly confesses and forsakes his sin finds mercy. "If we confess our sins he is faithful and just to forgive them," the apostle says. A person can never hope for pardon who will not confess his sin; how could he? As confession belongs to repentance, so if it's *right* confession, it will have a sight of sin, but in the context of sorrow, and shame which are joined to it. Men must make their confessions, having in their souls a great sorrow for having offended the King. There must be a great displeasure against

---

[28] Sometimes Scripture uses the term "humbled" for the whole act of repentance, "Wherefore the LORD brought upon them the captains of the host of the king of Assyria, which took Manasseh among the thorns, and bound him with fetters, and carried him to Babylon. And when he was in affliction, he besought the LORD his God, and *humbled himself greatly* before the God of his fathers," (2 Chron. 33:11-12).

themselves for their disobedience, but not merely because they are concerned *for themselves,* but that they are concerned they have *sinned against the King of heaven and his glory.* When the Apostle perceived the Corinthians to have fallen into a great sin, he wrote a sharp letter to them, and the consideration of that, and what they had done, worked in them the beginning of repentance, a godly sorrow, or sorrow according to God, which he requires, and will accept if it is sincere, according to the nature of the sin committed. This is *godly sorrow,* not *merely* sorrow. Godly sorrow is often given in Scripture for the *whole* of godly repentance.[29] The one who sins should be grieved, when he considers what he has done before the King's holy eyes and against his character. Scripture calls true repentance a broken heart, a contrite spirit. "...but to this man will I look, even to him that is poor and of a contrite spirit, and trembleth at my word," (Isa. 66:2).

In the Old Testament they used to express penitent sorrow and grief, by *wearing sackcloth,* and sitting in ashes. In the narrative of the King of Nineveh in that great affliction of soul which surprised him when Jonah preached it, he heard wrath was coming. He repented. To this also they joined fasting, acknowledging that by reason of their sins they were not worthy to eat, and so not to live; and when they did so, were said to afflict their souls. "Is it such a fast that I

---

[29] "For godly sorrow worketh repentance," (2 Cor. 7:10).

have chosen? a day for a man to afflict his soul? is it to bow down his head as a bulrush, and to spread sackcloth and ashes under him? wilt thou call this a fast, and an acceptable day to the LORD?" (Isa. 58:5). Do Christians speak like this or act like this today, or is it all *happy clappy*?

There must be a deep sense that one has of their sin, and how truly they are grieved that by it that they had offended God in his Kingly dominion over sin. You can hear it in the words of the penitent thief, "Lord, remember me when you come into your kingdom," as his life was expiring (Luke 23:42). People think such expressions of sorrow and shame are foolish, ancient, old timey, and such. Yet, I doubt, when such people are brought to be judged before the Great Tribunal of Christ the King, that they will think that way then. What are famous people, who died in their sins, that everyone looked up to, *thinking right now?* They are not thinking that repentance is *old timey*. Any kind of confession that a person makes without shame and sorrow for sin, will do him little good, and never lead him to turning. If it doesn't wound the heart, and cut to the quick, as in Acts 2 where it did for 3000, then the heart is still adamant stone. Sorrow must have shame as it attendant.

Adam and Eve were shamed for their sin. They were so ashamed that in their sin it made them *foolish* to think that leaves would cover them up. How could they think that *leaf coverings* would help them against divine fury? A person who sins thinks to be happy in a better way than that which God has directed him to, and is so foolish not to understand the sad consequences of his disobedience. The psalmist said, "Thy favour (lovingkindness) is better than life," or anything in it (Psalm 63:3).

This shame of a penitent sinner is heightened because he sees his ingratitude to God. This ingratitude is a great aggravation of the baseness of sin, that the prophet Isaiah, dumbfounded at it, cries out in God's behalf, "Hear O Heavens, give ear O Earth," (Isa. 1:2), why? "I have nourished and brought up children, and they have rebelled against me." Why? it follows, it's vile, so low that the beasts are not capable of it, "The ox knows his owner, and the ass his masters crib: but Israel doth not know, my people doth not consider," (Isa. 1:3). They do not have a discernable *sense* of sin and repentance, and they are worse than beasts. They do not have a sense of what it means to receive the kingdom, in their ingratitude towards the love of the Savior in dying for their sins; they see no need of it, until it's too late.

There must be attached to "shame and sorrow" in repentance, confession and the earnest prayer for pardon. Will God give over his kingdom to those that do not implore him to do so? It is fitting that the sinner should fall on his knees before the Eternal Father, and beg pardon from the King. It is to be done with fervency and zeal. "The effectual fervent prayer of a righteous man availeth much," James says. If a man prays lamely, what will he gain? Who is he addressing? Who is he petitioning? A sleepy, cold prayer freezes before it ever leaves the room. Could one imagine a cold prayer lifted up to Christ by the thief on the cross? Unthinkable. When such petitioning is cold, it shows that there is no sorrow or shame for what is being asked for; and one really doesn't know what he prays for. The penitent sinner is sensible of what he stands in need of, and how unworthy he is to receive it. He considers the greatness of the person of whom he begs it, and will pray with all possible earnestness for it. To strive earnestly in prayer, as Jacob did when he wrestled with the Angel, and would not let him go until he blessed him.

In repentance to the King to enter the kingdom there must be *hatred* of sin. Such a one will hate all things contrary to God's kingly character and will. And, they love all things in accordance with God's character and will. It is the duty of all pardoned souls to hate all sin as sin. There must be a love for what God loves, and a hatred for that which God hates. It is not enough to desire to reform. There must be a throwing off and putting on; a throwing off sin, and putting on Christ; a turning from sin and a turning to Christ.

Hypocrites, to some extent, can stop sin in its tracks, but they can't mortify it. They can stop walking into the bar. They can stop a lie from coming out of their mouth. But they do not see stopping sin as just, good and hold. They have no ability to get it out of their heart. They have no real victory over any sin to kill it. "You who love the LORD, hate evil!" (Psa. 97:10). *Hate evil.* New life in Jesus Christ, through the transforming power of the Spirit of God, changes their heart so that it not only chooses that which is good, but *abhors* that which is evil.[30] Any continued obstinance against God is sin. Any obstinance and rebellion against God's word is sin. To continue in it is a sign of condemnation not repentance; this is not what Christ said people must do to "gain" a kingdom. It is the duty of the Christian to hate all sin as sin; to repent. Whatever God hates, they are required to hate as well when they finish such a confession.

Then, in repentance to the King to enter the kingdom and receive his kingdom, there must be *turning* from sin. Repentance is a broken heart before God. Can this be done as lukewarm? Can it be done partially? Can it be done *only a little*? There is a change in the heart, there is a change in the soul, and there is change in the mind. It is a *whole* turning.

There is much more to godly repentance than a simple "confession", just mouthing words. 2 Timothy 2:25 speaks about God granting a conversion, "granting them repentance." The *form* of this word for *repentance* is used twenty-six times in the New Testament. In this

---

[30] We call this mortifying sin (killing it) and vivifying the spirit (making it alive) all by supernatural grace.

sense it never refers to anything less than a complete conversion; a turn.

Practically, repentance, then, is speedy, sincere and complete. It is done immediately and with all haste, which Jesus *expected*. Because if the Jews would not speedily repent as they heard his preaching, he would, in fulfilling the Old Testament, *turn to the Gentiles*.

If someone is in eternal danger, is it not reasonable to think that such a person will be sensible of the approaching danger, and will endeavor to prevent it as soon as he can? If a man's house is on fire, will he go back to sleep in the room, or escape? Delaying in this makes the work harder, for it piles up more sin and endangers the person. Pardon is not about *whenever* a person desires to do it. Christ said repent, the kingdom is at hand, and so he required an *immediate* response. Men are commanded to, "seek the Lord while he may be found," and, "those that seek me early shall find me." Can sin, which has taken deep root in the soul, be cast out easily? Why would one think it to be so easy as to wait, or put it off? This waiting was not what Christ expected. Can a man's unwillingness to do it speedily be seen in the mortification of sin in an instant? The longer it sits, the worse it gets, and the stronger sin becomes. There should be no delay to believe the preaching of the King.

If repentance is enacted by sight, sorrow, confession, shame, hatred and turning, speedily with sincerity, and universally, one shall receive a whole kingdom, and receive Christ the King, who will dwell in them. For, repentance is required to enter into the kingdom of heaven, and to receive it.

What is the way and means to gain a life of repentance? "A life of it," you think, "I thought it was only once?" To enter life, repentance is required by the King. To work anything pleasing in God's sight, works worthy of true repentance, is the *continued desire* of all Christians. It must be cultivated, not for a continued entrance into the kingdom, but then to show forth that one is in the kingdom, and that the kingdom is in them; that he serves the King with reverence and godly fear.[31]

If you *really* turn from sin, you have no return to it. Hosea 14:8, "Ephraim shall say, what have I to do *any more* with idols?" When men return to sins they have forsaken, they become like a dog returning to its vomit, the wise man said. Thomas Watson in his book on repentance quoted Isadore who believed, "Some have become converts to the Christian faith, and to have turned from sin, but they have returned to their sins again. This is a returning to folly." Such a return to the wayward life of sin may not be an evidence of true conversion, but spurious faith or even apostacy. He is sinning against the illuminations of the Spirit and the

---

[31] "Wherefore we receiving a kingdom which cannot be moved, let us have grace, whereby we may serve God acceptably with reverence and godly fear: for our God is a consuming fire," (Heb. 12:28-29).

dominion of King Jesus. Thomas Watson said, "A true turning from sin, is a divorcing it, so as never to come near it any more: and whoever is in this way turned from sin is a blessed person, Acts 3:26, "God having raised up his Son Jesus, sent him to bless you, in turning every one of you from his iniquities."[32] This could cause a person to tremble knowing they have sin which so easily besets them.

What we mean here is that the *habitual life* of sin is over. Now sin is surprising in the saint. Now it is *surprising* in you. You fall into a sin, and if anyone does, we have an advocate with the Father, Jesus Christ the righteous one (1 John 2:1). You then look for forgiveness, and desire repentance to be renewed against the decaying body of remaining sin in you. But it is *surprising to you* when it materializes. "How did that happen?" you think. "Why did I do that again?" you think. It is never *normal*, and always detestable. It's not planned, and you don't go out of your way to go and sin because you want to act the same way you did when you were not a Christian. A change has been made, and now striving to enter the kingdom by violence is a constant course. Sin is *no longer* a constant course. You have new priorities, and that is to please your Savior.

Are you not thoroughly ashamed to sin against King Jesus? When you consent to sin, to throw yourself out of the joy of the Lord, that tranquility of mind in

---

[32] Watson, Thomas, *The Doctrine of Repentance*, (London: R.W., 1668), 69–70.

peace with God, into grief, such is a terrible uncomfortable path? You know what it is like when you see how by sin you debased yourself, you lose honor, dignity, pleasure, virtue, for some façade of satisfaction in the flesh of some kind, and indulging some vile affection and sin, you think? You quench the Spirit's work. You cover the candle with the snuffer, if you will, trying to put out the bright light of the Spirit. I find that to be one of the most graphic *secular* depictions of this thought by the fictional character Scrooge in trying to snuff out the light of the illuminating Ghost of Christmas past in Dicken's novel, *A Christmas Carol*. "What!" exclaimed the Ghost, "would you so soon put out, with worldly hands, the light I give?" You can hear the Spirit of God screaming that to the church all through Scripture. "Would you so quickly, in sin, put out my illuminating light? Why would you want to grieve me and vex me and partake in sin, when the blessings of Jesus Christ will make you infinitely happy?" You must think, "Do I please myself with committing sin, when my Savior in pure love suffered so much pain with infinite amazements on the cross for it? What am I? Am I so corrupt as to trample under my feet the blood of the Son of God, and to mock the prayers and tears of my Savior? Do I long to put out the light of the Spirit of truth by my worldly hands, heart, and mind?" Be spiritually persuaded that those who *persist in a corrupt course*, without repentance and without turning from it to King Jesus, will *perish*. For in

Christ's preaching he said, "except ye repent, ye shall all likewise perish," (Luke 13:3).

You must live within the sphere of sincere repentance always; it is the holy disposition of those in Christ's kingdom, and who have the kingdom in them. Scripture calls it the "renewing of the mind," "crucifying the old man and his deeds," "putting off the body of sin" and destroying it, "crucifying the flesh with the affections and lusts," "purging ourselves from all filthiness of flesh and spirit," and "perfecting holiness in the fear of God."

Are you a new creature? Jesus says, then, and exhorts you, *act like it.* Go and sin no more (John 8:11). Being made new creatures and partakers of a divine nature, well then, act in accordance with *godliness*. A new creature, a change in your apprehension and a changed view of all of life is your disposition now. You live in a new kingdom by faith under the King; and are to *act* like new creatures. You must have a constant alteration of your affections to *his* holy will. It is the only way of entrance into it and the only way of living to it and him. You are convinced of the necessity of the King's continued good favor, and the excellency of holiness, the reasonableness of Christ's imputed virtue, and the necessary connection which is between holiness and happiness. Your affections are now repentantly different. Those who are Christs, have "crucified the flesh with its affections and lusts," and "have put off the old man," which is corrupt according to the deceitful lusts. You have a new heart, you have another spirit, like Caleb and Joshua, (Num. 14:24). The heart of stone is broken in pieces, and being cast away, one of flesh is put in its place. You know it if you have it; and you don't know it if you don't. Such a heart is soft and pliable to the will of the King. That which was stiff necked, now stoops over to take up the yoke Christ places on it with happiness. Now you say with Christ, "Not my will, O Father, but thine be done: that which pleases you shall please me in all things."

And all the sincerity of true repentance which gains an entrance into the kingdom, declares itself in outward expressions which answer the profession made to the King. New life means you are a new man. That is, to do works agreeable to the nature of the thing itself and its profession. Walk in the Spirit, live according to that new nature, and let the power of heavenly doctrine shine forth in the beauty of holy conversation. You acknowledge Christ for your King and you desire to do what the King commands you.

If you continue in this state and course of your life, such a sincere repentant life will show itself in its perseverance. Lactantius said, "That to repent is to profess and affirm that we will sin no more."[33] Or as the King said, "If you continue in my words, (*i.e.* the obedience of my doctrine), you shall be my disciples indeed," (John 8:31). Such obedience requires great honesty of intention in you, and the simplicity of heart

---

[33] *The Divine Institutes*, Lib. 6, chapter 13, *of mercy*.

in your desire to stick close to the throne of the King. Christ said that he who puts his hand to the heavenly plough, and does not renounce what may make him look back after he has begun, is not fit for the kingdom of God (Luke 9:62). If you hold the plough, and keep looking back, all your lines will be crooked in the dirt; it will be a terrible plough job. And so, he tells us not to mix ourselves with the world. He says, "Remember Lot's wife," (Luke 17:32), signifying to us plainly enough, that such as have forsaken Sodom and their sins, must not look back with yearning eyes on worldly things.

Sincere repentance speaks in this way:

"O Lord, I have sinned against you, but I repent, and you know the depth of my heart, and know that I repent truly. You know all things. You know I love you. In your sacred presence I make my vow that I will obey you. I will observe what my duty is before your Kingly holiness. And where these duties fail, I will read carefully the gospel of your kingdom, and what I find there to be your will, shall be to me an indispensable law. I make this solemn declaration, that I will keep no enemy of yours in my soul; and if I find anything lurking there which may displease you, let me know my heart by your instruction, and I will cast it out by the Spirit. I desire to be in your sight a faithful and victorious soldier in

> Christ's army, indeed, and pray that I may inherit the blessing which you bestow on those in whose spirit is no guile. Try me, O God, and seek the ground of my heart; prove me, and examine my thoughts; look well if there is any way of wickedness in me, and lead me in the way everlasting."

Such is said and held with an honest intention and a firm resolution, proposing action.

And yet, "Not as though I had already attained, either were already perfect: but I follow after, if that I may apprehend that for which also I am apprehended of Christ Jesus. ... I count not myself to have apprehended: but this one thing I do, forgetting those things which are behind, and reaching forth unto those things which are before, I press toward the mark for the prize of the high calling of God in Christ Jesus. Let us therefore, as many as be perfect, be thus minded: and if in any thing ye be otherwise minded, God shall reveal even this unto you. Nevertheless, whereto we have already attained, let us walk by the same rule, let us mind the same thing," (Phil. 3:12-16). And also, "Wherefore since we are receiving a kingdom which cannot be moved, let us have grace, whereby we may serve God acceptably with reverence and godly fear," (Heb. 12:28-29), for repentance is required by King Jesus to enter into the kingdom of heaven, and for it to enter into you.

Chapter 3: King Jesus' Requirement for Kingdom Entry

In the next chapter we will consider the *atonement* of the kingdom in Jesus' preaching.

Chapter 4:
God's Reign as King in Christ's Substitutionary Atonement

"From that time Jesus began to preach, and to say, Repent: for the kingdom of heaven is at hand," (Matt. 4:17).

Jesus preached to declare the mind and intention of the Father, as God's Divine Messenger and Herald, the Son of Man, the Great Exegete of the Father, to declare him (John 1:18). In his first sermon, as with his forerunner John, he preached *God's kingdom* and *repentance*; he preached God's gospel.

As a reminder, to preach the kingdom involves the King and his will. God is absolute King over the universe; governing everything. He is particular as King in his government of his church. He rules over the fall as King, and can reverse the fall. He does this through his *covenant*. He does this through his Mediator of the covenant. He does this through the Christ, who is the divine and all powerful Son of Man.

To preach the kingdom is to preach about *entry* into the kingdom. Jesus required an immediate response to preaching the kingdom, the King and the dominion of the King over all. His hearers knew about the dominion of God, repentance, and the kingdom of the Great King; that God required repentance. "Repent," John the Baptist says, (Matt. 3:2), "for the kingdom of heaven is at hand." The world to come is *coming upon you*. And Christ says, Mark 1:14, "Repent, for the kingdom of heaven is at hand," and Matt. 16:28, "There are some that stand here that shall not taste of death till they see the Son of Man come in his kingdom." That is the manner and outward circumstance of the church of the Old Testament, now abolished, and the church under the *new testator*, that is King Jesus, is ready to take place by the Son of Man's coming, therefore, *repent and receive these truths about the King and his kingdom.*

Repentance is in light of the fall, and the waywardness of men in their desire to be rebels instead of servants. Repentance, therefore, includes repentance from sin, in light of God's holy law and providence over sinful men. It is an evangelical grace, a supernatural grace, that is required speedily for entrance into the kingdom, and for the kingdom to reside in men.

To gain repentance, from the King, in his dominion over the fall, is to gain it by God's good pleasure, and in *his way*, and in no other way. But, to gain such supernatural repentance is only by the substitutionary atonement of his Mediator. It is not possible to gain it in any other way. Is this what Christ considered in his preaching of the Old Testament, and is this what the Scriptures bear out? As much as Jonah did not walk through Nineveh merely saying, "Yet forty days and Nineveh shall be overthrown." Did Nineveh repent? Why, *yes*, the people there did. How did they repent if they did not know *what repentance was?* Were they instructed in those few words which Jonah said, "to repent." Jesus did not merely walk into a town and say "repent for the kingdom of heaven is at hand," and then turn away and walk out. His words are *short hand* for his preaching, which contained many truths. "To whom also he shewed himself alive after his passion by many infallible proofs, being seen of them forty days, and speaking of the things pertaining to the kingdom of God," (Acts 1:3). *Things*, plural. One of those *things*, having set down the *what* and *why* of the gospel, is to more fully deal with the *how* of the gospel. *How* does the King reign? God's particular reign as King is expressed in Christ's substitutionary atonement and its application to penitent and believing sinners. This concerns the *how* of the good tidings of the gospel.

God is the *who* of the gospel, his kingdom is the *what* of the gospel, the fall reversing power of God in men is the exercise of the *why* of the gospel, and the work and merit of the Christ in his life and atonement (and all things gathered from that idea) is the *how* of those good tidings.[1] Repentance required to gain access to the kingdom, surrounds repenting from sin; but this can only be done if certain requirements are met, and satisfaction to God's justice is appeased, otherwise, there is no salvation, and no ability to repent.[2]

---

[1] If preachers would simply understand this, the people of God would be more informed in their grasp and perception of Gospel truths!

Consider first, the nature of sin. What does it do? Original sin makes men guilty and necessitates punishment because it is hated by God.[3] It is a debt which all men are bound to pay to divine justice as a result of the fall. Original sin was reckoned to man's account by God because of Adam's transgression under the Covenant of Works. "...for in the day that thou eatest thereof thou shalt surely die," (Gen. 2:17). "But they like Adam have transgressed the covenant: there have they dealt treacherously against me," (Hosea 6:7). All men are bound up under this terrible plight.

Sin is *enmity* against God, which makes men *God haters* at conception, even if they deny it. "Behold, I was shapen in iniquity; and in sin did my mother conceive me," (Psa. 51:5). "...visiting the iniquity of the fathers upon the children unto the third and fourth generation of them that hate me," (Exod. 20:5), God says these things. Conceived human embryos in the womb begin life with a cosmic crime against God as God-haters. Why? "And God saw that the wickedness of man was great in the earth, and that every imagination of the thoughts of his heart was only evil continually," (Gen. 6:5). To repent, then, is *impossible* without God's help

---

[2] "...if God peradventure will give them repentance to the acknowledging of the truth," (2 Tim. 2:25).
[3] "Hate the evil, and love the good" (Amo. 5:15). "...for every abomination to the LORD, which he hateth, have they done unto their gods; for even their sons and their daughters they have burnt in the fire to their gods," (Deut. 12:31). "The LORD trieth the righteous: but the wicked and him that loveth violence his soul hateth," (Psalm 11:5).

because men are dead in sin, God-haters.[4] To enter the kingdom is impossible without God's saving and regenerating hand to save them. "And I will give them one heart, and I will put a new spirit within you; and I will take the stony heart out of their flesh, and will give them an heart of flesh," (Eze. 11:19). Who does this? *God* does this. Men in this sinful state, deserve death, and deserve damnation at God's hand because of the fall of Adam reckoned to their account. They have sinned against God by cosmic treason, "Whosoever hath sinned against me, him will I blot out of my book," (Exod. 32:33). "The LORD will not spare him, but then the anger of the LORD and his jealousy shall smoke against that man, and all the curses that are written in this book shall lie upon him, and the LORD shall blot out his name from under heaven," (Deut. 29:20). But, "Blessed is the man unto whom the LORD imputeth not iniquity," (Psa. 32:2) and how does that happen?

In order to have sin *not* imputed, there must be something or someone that goes between the sinner and God. There must be a payment of the debt contracted by sin, the appeasing of divine wrath, and the expiation of guilt. The *sin debt* is a wage that God will pay in righteousness and justice, that which is owed to God. "...the soul that sinneth, it shall die," (Ezek. 18:4). What is owed to God is *complete perfection* in character and conduct. So, appeasing God's wrath

---

[4] "But he that sinneth against me wrongeth his own soul: all they that hate me love death," (Prov. 8:36).

against sin must take place; something must satisfy God. And in this satisfaction, God is able to justify sinners who come to him by this satisfaction. "...by his knowledge shall my righteous servant justify many; for he shall bear their iniquities," (Isa. 53:11). Guilt must be removed. "Then will I sprinkle clean water upon you, and ye shall be clean: from all your filthiness, and from all your idols, will I cleanse you," (Ezek. 36:25).

Consider second, the Judge of the earth must be satisfied. If the Judge of all the earth must be appeased, something or someone must appease him. "He shall see of the travail of his soul, and shall be satisfied: by his knowledge shall my righteous servant justify many; for he shall bear their iniquities," (Isa. 53:11). What does it mean to bear another's iniquities? Man cannot do it; he's wicked and evil. Someone *perfect* must do it in order to satisfy it. Whoever does it must do it out of grace and love, and infinitely so. Whoever does it must meet the requirements, and offer something that will satisfy the Great King who reigns in heaven as the infinite God of righteousness.

Justice must be exercised by the King against sin, and mercy must be given to the sinner so that the sinner may then be able to repent. For this to occur, an atonement must be made to divine justice by a Surety, and then God will mercifully pardon all those for whom the Surety gives his life. Through the mercy of God some men may be forgiven and exempt from punishment, by the substitution of a *surety* in their stead. He shall justify *many*. "Unto Adam also and to his wife did the LORD God make coats of skins, and clothed them," (Gen. 3:21). Why did he do this? Even at the first sin, the King killed the animals instead of killing the rebels. The animals were a *substitution* for them right from the very start. All Old Testament sacrifices are object lessons for sinners who *see* and understand the lesson. The ground of their effectiveness is the substitutionary atonement of the Christ for them; his work and death and merit uphold all types gone before him. "Thou in thy mercy hast led forth the people which thou hast redeemed," (Exod. 15:13). How are they redeemed but by the Christ? "He that covereth his sins shall not prosper: but whoso confesseth and forsaketh them shall have mercy," (Prov. 28:13). How will they have mercy in confessing and forsaking sin, but by Christ? The One making atonement must be considered. The One who makes atonement must be able to make a payment for the debt. It is an infinite debt. It is an affront to infinite holiness. It is an affront to God's infinite character. It is an affront to the King's infinite law.[5]

    The Christ must be designated a Mediator of God to fulfill all the stipulations of the covenant on behalf of those represented. In this he is to be both priest and sacrifice, to substitute himself in man's stead, and make atonement, by enduring the penal

---

[5] This is the reason that hell is *eternal* punishment against sinners. Their sins are infinite in relation to the law, and character of God.

sanction of the law. He must have the nature of those he represents, and so in this way he is both God and man. He must be God. He must be man. He must have the ability to offer a sacrifice of infinite value, against both God's nature, which is infinite, and man's nature that has sinned against God where those sins gain an infinite penalty. Without a sacrifice appealing to the human nature, it would never be accepted, for the blood of bulls and goats does not save (Hebrews 10:4), they are only *types* in the Old Testament of the Christ to come. Without a sacrifice that could be infinite in its perfection *and* nature, it would never satisfy an infinite divine fury and an infinite justice.

    Christ had a common nature with men, that sin would be punished in the same nature which it was guilty. "And I will put enmity between thee and the woman, and between thy seed and her seed; it shall bruise thy head, and thou shalt bruise his heel," (Gen. 3:15). "Therefore will he give them up, until the time that she which travaileth hath brought forth: then the remnant of his brethren shall return unto the children of Israel," (Micah 5:3). He had a consent to do the act. By the consent of his will, that he should voluntarily take the burden on himself to do this for them. "Then said I, Lo, I come: in the volume of the book it is written of me, I delight to do thy will, O my God: yea, thy law is within my heart," (Psa. 40:7-8). He must have power to do this act. "Therefore will I divide him a portion with the great, and he shall divide the spoil with the strong;

because he hath poured out his soul unto death: and he was numbered with the transgressors; and he bare the sin of many, and made intercession for the transgressors," (Isa. 53:12). He must have power to bear God's wrath against sin. "Surely he hath borne our griefs, and carried our sorrows: yet we did esteem him stricken, smitten of God, and afflicted. But he was wounded for our transgressions, he was bruised for our iniquities: the chastisement of our peace was upon him; and with his stripes we are healed," (Isa. 53:4-5). He must be able by way of offering to give that which God requires, which would be accomplished in perfect holiness, without blemish. "...because he had done no violence, neither was any deceit in his mouth," (Isa. 53:9). In all this he fulfills all things required by God, and that willingly as God's fellow in *covenant* with the Father. "...the man that is my fellow," (Zech. 13:7). "...and this is his name whereby he shall be called, *(what is the name of Christ above every name?)* THE LORD OUR RIGHTEOUSNESS," (Jer. 23:6).

    The preaching of the kingdom and repentance by the Christ announces his brutal and excruciating death, confirming the necessity of this work and the merit needed, bound up throughout all of the Scriptures; Christ means *all this* when he says *the kingdom of heaven is at hand*. "And thou shalt make a mercy seat of pure gold," (Exod. 25:17), Christ is the mercy seat on which the blood of the everlasting covenant is poured out on. He alone is able to confirm the sacrifice and offer to God that which God requires: to declare the righteousness of God in the work needed, that men might repent and be admitted into a kingdom that they could never have otherwise. "Mercy and truth are met together; righteousness and peace have kissed each other," (Psa. 85:10), this is in the Christ. "And the work of righteousness shall be peace; and the effect of righteousness quietness and assurance for ever," (Isa. 32:17), again, in the Christ. "...the chastisement of our peace was upon him; and with his stripes we are healed," (Isa. 53:5), again, *by the Christ*. The truth of the atonement is very clear, even in this cursory view.

Christ has redeemed men by the price of his blood. This is an interesting argument to make here. Those religious pundits who reject this "substitutionary" idea do so because they say Christ had *not yet gone to the cross*, but was preaching *repentance* for kingdom entrance. He sent out his disciples to preach as well, telling them that they ought to preach that the kingdom of God is at hand, to repent. He did not tell them to preach his atonement, or that Jesus would at some point die on a cross, did he? This is because this idea of atonement is bound up in the idea of *the King, his kingdom, his reconciliation to God, his peace making, his blood shedding, his sacrifice, his fulfillment of all types, his bringing in the coming of the kingdom in its fullness, his covenant*; to say preach "the kingdom," and all things in the, "kingdom," is to preach the *who*, the *what*, the *why* and the *how* of the Christ. Not merely mouth a few words. To miss that, and make the false teacher's assertion that Christ did not have in mind *an atonement* in that preaching, is to lead men astray with a devilish lie; they err not knowing the Scriptures. "But now thus saith the LORD that created thee, O Jacob, and he that formed thee, O Israel, Fear not: for I have redeemed thee, I have called thee by thy name; thou art mine," (Isa. 43:1), this is as much about the kingdom in atonement, as preaching about the King or the need to repent.

Christ redeemed men by the blood of the atonement made for them. "...he is brought as a lamb to the slaughter," (Isa. 53:7). "...I gave my back to the smiters..." (Isa. 50:6). "...when thou shalt make his soul an offering for sin," (Isa. 53:10). "...I will save them ... wherein they have sinned, and will cleanse them," (Ezek. 37:23). "...to make an atonement for your souls," (Exod. 30:15). "...to make an atonement for all Israel," (2 Chron. 29:24). His very name is substitutionary in its work. "...and with him is *plenteous redemption*. And he shall redeem Israel from all his iniquities," (Psa. 130:7-8). "...and this is his name whereby he shall be called, THE LORD OUR RIGHTEOUSNESS," (Jer. 23:6). All of this is *substitutionary* language. The Old Testament is a substitutionary testament ... but so is the New.

Christ died on behalf of his people to save them and make atonement for them. "...and to make an end of sins, and to make reconciliation for iniquity, and to bring in everlasting righteousness, and to seal up the vision and prophecy, and to anoint the most Holy," (Dan. 9:24). Christ died for his people vicariously; suffering in the place of another. "...he hath borne our griefs," (Isa. 53:4). "...for the transgression of my people was he stricken," (Isa. 53:8). "And if a man have committed a sin worthy of death, and he be to be put to death, and thou hang him on a tree," (Deut. 21:22). What sin did the Christ have? None. But "...he that is hanged is accursed of God;" (Deut. 21:23). Christ was accursed for his people on behalf of others. "...they that be cursed of him shall be cut off," (Psa. 37:22). He was cursed by bearing his people's sins. The sins are borne by him being bruised and wounded, sin laid on him as the atoning sacrifice. Christ took on himself and suffered the punishment of sin; he took on the punishment of the transgressors. Making his soul an offering, and laid down his life an offering for sin, bore sin in the manner of a criminal. A, "lamb of the first year without blemish for a sin offering," (Num. 6:14). In his offering, "he was bruised for our iniquities," (Isa. 53:5). "...the suffering of punishment due to sin, "he hath borne our griefs, and carried our sorrows," (verse 4), ...the imputation of sins to Christ by God as a judge for his people, "the Lord laid on him the iniquity of us all," (verse 6), ...his voluntary undertaking as surety, "he was oppressed and afflicted, yet he opened not his mouth," he did not refuse to bear them, (verse 8), ...an expiation for sin and a full payment of the debt, "yet it pleased the Lord to bruise him, he hath put him to grief: when thou shalt make his soul on offering for sin" (verse 10). Isaiah's prophecy was fulfilled, "the chastisement of our peace was *upon* him;" (Isa. 53:5). This is all bound up in substitutionary language.

Why is Christ called the High Priest but to offer sacrifice? He, "...makes his soul an offering for sin," (Isa. 53:10). He is a priest in all these covenantal acts pertaining to God, to appease him by an atoning sacrifice. He is a priest on behalf of those criminals against both God and him for whom he would die. He propitiates God's wrath. He expiates sin. He pardons and allows entrance of penitent sinners into his kingdom. In this, sinners find reconciliation with God, peace with God. "...to make reconciliation for them, saith the Lord GOD," (Ezek. 45:15). "...to make reconciliation for iniquity," (Dan. 9:24). And such a reconciliation is effected, "by making peace through his sacrifice," by an atoning sacrifice. Francis Turretin said, "The law, indeed, demands that the person who sins shall suffer, but the gospel, through the fatherly kindness of God, declares it necessary that there shall be a substitution, that it suffices to punish sin, and let the sinner go free."[6] That the King sent the Mediator, because of sin and the fall, and the Mediator *mediates*. He is the *go between* and offers that which allows God to declare people righteous, on no account of their doing,

---

[6] Turretin, Francis, eBook, *The Substitutionary Atonement of Jesus Christ*, (Coconut Creek, FL: Puritan Publications, 2014), chapter 2 section 6.

or will or work or merit ... *or anything*. The whole Old Testament is a divine picture of substitutionary sacrifice. It teaches sinners *how* the King has saved rebels through the Christ.

Is not this atonement, not astonishing on behalf of sinners in light of divine mercy? He makes them upright by his work, "...no good thing will he withhold from them that walk uprightly," (Psa. 84:11). That includes giving his Son on the cross. He has perfectly satisfied divine justice for all his people's sins. He did this by the one offering of atonement, not only for their guilt, but also for all punishment which may be due them, both temporal and eternal. When Jesus dies, he brings in the kingdom. He died either for all the sins of all men, which is universalism. Or, he died for some of the sins of all men, which is Roman Catholicism. Or he died for all of the sins of some men, and that is the *how* of the gospel.[7] There are no more offerings to be made for sin; what he did, he did, and what he fulfilled is complete. It is perfect in every way, without blemish. "...he shall offer it without blemish before the LORD," (Lev. 3:1). It was accomplished in infinite degree. "...it shall be perfect to be accepted; there shall be no blemish therein," (Lev. 22:21). It was perfect in its effects. "...to bring in everlasting righteousness," (Dan. 9:24). "Behold, I give unto him my covenant of peace," (Num. 25:12). And of the Christ, the Lord says, "Thou

---

[7] See John Owen's work, *The Death of Death in the Death of Christ*, Volume 10 of his *Works*, for a full discussion of this idea.

art a priest for ever," (Psa. 110:4), in this work of *atonement.*

Did God approve of this Christ and his work? "For thou wilt not leave my soul in hell; neither wilt thou suffer thine Holy One to see corruption," (Psa. 16:10). Of course he did, and he *resurrected* him. "That he should still live for ever, and not see corruption," (Psa. 49:9). "Behold, my servant shall deal prudently, he shall be exalted and extolled, and be very high," (Isa. 52:13). In his exaltation he is lifted up, and God accepts his atoning work on behalf of all those for whom he died.

And what will he do? "For thus saith the high and lofty One that inhabiteth eternity, whose name is Holy; I dwell in the high and holy place, with him also that is of a contrite and humble spirit, to revive the spirit of the humble, and to revive the heart of the contrite ones," (Isa. 57:15). He will open the kingdom of heaven, and hold it out to all who repent, and turn to him; to revive their heart, to change them, to renew them. "But they that wait upon the LORD shall renew their strength; they shall mount up with wings as eagles; they shall run, and not be weary; and they shall walk, and not faint," (Isa. 40:31). It is a glorious salvation, where God's particular reign as King is seen in the substitutionary atonement of the Son of Man for his people.

Now, take a moment, and consider, *what have you not heard here?* Think about this chapter so far, and consider, there was not a single verse here from the

Chapter 4: Christ's Substitutionary Atonement

New Testament. What does the *Old Testament teach* that the New Testament doesn't? What does the *New Testament teach* that the Old Testament doesn't? What did Jesus think about the King, his dominion, his kingdom, his conditions, his atonement, his preaching to open the way to God to sinners who may come freely and drink from the waters of eternal life in the Spirit? Clement (AD 90) said, "Because of the love he felt for us, Jesus Christ our Lord gave his blood for us by the will of God, his body for our bodies, and his soul for our souls."[8] Substitutionary language. Ignatius (AD 107) said, "Now, He suffered all these things for our sakes, that we might be saved."[9] Substitutionary language. Eusebius of Caesarea (AD 275-339) said, "Thus the Lamb of God, that taketh away the sins of the world, became a curse on our behalf. ... And the Lamb of God not only did this, but was chastised on our behalf, and suffered a penalty He did not owe, but which we owed because of the multitude of our sins; and so He became the cause of the forgiveness of our sins, because He received death for us, and transferred to Himself the scourging, the insults, and the dishonour, which were due to us, and drew down upon Himself the appointed curse, being made a curse for us. ... But since being in the likeness of sinful flesh He condemned sin in the

---

[8] Clement of Alexandris (AD 90), Clement, First Epistle of Clement to the Corinthians 49, in The Ante-Nicene Fathers, eds. Alexander Roberts and James Donaldson, 10 vols. (Peabody, Mass: Hendrickson, 1994) 1:18.
[9] Ignatius, *Epistle of Ignatius to the Smyrnaeans*, 2, ANF 1:87.

flesh, the words quoted are rightly used. And in that He made our sins His own from His love and benevolence towards us."[10] Substitutionary language. Shall I quote Gottshalk, Anslem, Wycliffe, John Calvin, Martin Luther, all the good puritans, the Dutch reformers, the creeds the catechisms, the confessions, Jonathan Edwards, George Whitefield, the Princeton theologians ... who shall be quoted? *All good teachers throughout the history of the Christian church teach the substitutionary atonement of Jesus Christ.* Never forget that.

Shall it be proved in this from the New Testament? Is there *really a need* to prove this out in the New Testament? "Even as the Son of man came not to be ministered unto, but to minister, and to give his life a ransom for many," (Matt. 20:28). Jesus said this, as a clarification of his preaching, as he did with almost everything he said. "Whom God hath set forth to be a propitiation through faith in his blood, to declare his righteousness for the remission of sins that are past, through the forbearance of God," (Rom. 3:25). "But this man, after he had offered one sacrifice for sins for ever, sat down on the right hand of God," (Heb. 10:12). God sending, "his Son to be the propitiation for our sins," (1 John 4:10). "...even Jesus, which delivered us from the wrath to come," (1 Thess. 1:10). "Jesus Christ of the seed of David was raised from the dead," (2 Tim. 2:8). "God,

---

[10] Demonstratio Evangelica 10.1, trans. W. J. Ferrar, http://www.earlychristianwritings.com/fathers/eusebius_de_12_book10.html (accessed June 29, 2009).

Chapter 4: Christ's Substitutionary Atonement

that raised him up from the dead, and gave him glory," (1 Peter 1:21). "He that descended is the same also that ascended up far above all heavens," (Eph. 4:10). "God also hath highly exalted him," (Phil. 2:9). What do all these things teach? What did John the Baptist teach? What did Jesus teach? What did his apostles, and his prophets, and what should his ministers preach? They taught the *Old Testament*. They taught *substitutionary atonement*. They taught the *kingdom*. They taught the *gospel*.

Consider all this strung together in this way: "I saw in the night visions, and, behold, one like the Son of man came with the clouds of heaven, ["he was taken up; and a cloud received him out of their sight," (Acts 1:9)], and he came to the Ancient of days, and they brought him near before him. And there was given him dominion, and glory, and a kingdom, [seeing also the Christ sitting upon a throne, high and lifted up, and his train filled the temple. Above it stood the seraphims: each one had six wings; with twain he covered his face, and with twain he covered his feet, and with twain he did fly. And one cried unto another, and said, Holy, holy, holy, is the LORD of hosts: the whole earth is full of his glory," (Isa. 6:1-3).] that all people, nations, and languages, should serve him: [And there was a voice from the firmament ... above the firmament ... was the likeness of a throne, ... and upon the likeness of the throne was the likeness as the appearance of a man above upon it. I saw as it were the appearance of fire, and it had brightness round about ... so was the appearance of the brightness round about. [And his raiment became shining, exceeding white as snow] (Mark 9:3). This was the appearance of the likeness of the glory of the LORD. And when I saw it, I fell upon my face, and I heard a voice of one that spake," (Ezek. 1:25-28)] his dominion is an everlasting dominion, which shall not pass away, and his kingdom that which shall not be destroyed," (Dan. 7:13-14). His kingdom is an everlasting kingdom, and his dominion endureth throughout all generations. He upholds all that fall, and raiseth up all those that be bowed down," (Psa. 145:13-14). All these things are bound up in Christ's substitutionary atonement and his words, "Repent, for the kingdom of heaven is at hand." All this is meant, *and more*, in what Christ preached.

What, then, is the application of the substitutionary atonement of Christ to sinners? To keep close to the preaching of Christ, repentance is the entrance to the kingdom of heaven, and the kingdom to enter sinners. If repentance is the entrance, and bound up in the preaching of Christ in the work of his substitutionary atonement, the application of which is by the work of the Spirit, as we have seen, then entrance into heaven is not by works, but by granted repentance, which is a result of Christ's work, applied by the Spirit to the undeserving and miserable.

Christ is a substitution for poor sinners. Sin is a debt to God, it is enmity against him, and it is a crime against his character. Someone has to pay; either the rebel pays, who does not get out of prison until he pays the last penny, which is impossible, or a Savior has to pay. What does God require? The blood of bulls and goats don't save, as Hebrews 10:4 says. There must be a desire to fulfill all that God requires willingly. "Lo, I come to do thy will," (Heb. 10:9), Christ says, "I will do it Father, I will pay for them." The sacrifice must be perfect, in holiness, without sin, to substitute himself for his people, (Heb. 7:25-27).

The sacrifice of Christ alone is the only sacrifice on its own account, acceptable to God, that allows sinners entrance into the kingdom. Sacrifices are those which are offered to God, where its suffering and death makes atonement and secures acceptance for all those that have it offered for them. In the substitution for the sinner, a double cure takes place. God's wrath is appeased, and the sin of the individual is taken away. Jesus does that, apart from anything or anyone.

You might say, "but wait, were there not sacrifices, substitutionary sacrifices offered in the Old Testament on behalf of sinners?" Of course, and that was the point, all these were *types* of the great sacrifice of Christ to come. And yet the objection goes on, "Don't we see that people brought sacrifices and they were not consumed? Was God not pleased with those sacrifices?" The lamb slaughtered as a sacrifice and roasted in the fire (of God's wrath) is substituted in the sinner's place; what kind of picture is that? What object lesson is that? What should have happened to the sinner, happens to the lamb: death, and hell happens to the lamb, killed and *roasted in the fire (2 Chron. 35:13)*. It was a picture to remind them of sin; an object lesson of the most graphic sort. It was a picture to keep in their memory, time after time after time, to show them what they required to be in order to be accepted before God. Blood, death, blood, death, blood, death. The sacrifice is credited to the believing sinner by faith in God's means, by repentance. But the sacrifices of the Old Testament were not in and of themselves acceptable to God, for they never atoned for a single thing. What can the blood of bulls and goats do? "For it is not possible that the blood of bulls and of goats should take away sins," (Heb. 10:4). There was no moral goodness in them, they had no ability to appease God. Jonathan Edwards said, "They did not nor could not make atonement for the soul; they made no satisfaction to divine justice."[11] He is correct. They could do nothing. They were not offered *in the nature* of the human rebel, being goats and lambs and doves.

Why did God institute such things, then, for the church at that time? In these sacrifices, they were taught by God the necessity of God's justice needing to be satisfied by suffering of the penalty of sin; he was

---

[11] Jonathan Edwards, "The Sacrifice of Christ Acceptable," in *Sermons and Discourses, 1723–1729*, ed. Harry S. Stout and Kenneth P. Minkema, Volume 14, *The Works of Jonathan Edwards*, (New Haven; London: Yale University Press, 1997), 445.

teaching them the substitutionary atonement that would come in the Messiah. It was to show, by way of shadows and types, the sacrifice of Christ to come. "Yet it pleased the LORD to bruise him; he hath put him to grief: when thou shalt make his soul an offering for sin," (Isa. 53:10). They were to have a life of humble walking with God. Is this not what God requires? He requires a life of repentance, by faith in what God would do through the Mediator to come; and if they could do this, they could be saved. But who can do it under the dominion of the fall? Some *other dominion* must shine forth to render an atonement for such sinners in a manner befitting God, to satisfy God's righteousness.

So, the King himself came, he drew near, and the Son of Man gave his life as a ransom for many; *God with us*. What you do not have as a sinner, you become covered by the Christ who dies for you, where God now only sees the Christ covering you, that which is lovely, beautiful and perfect; and there *the kingdom is upon you*, the rule and reign of God in the Christ comes to you and in you and you in it. Christ's righteous fulfillment of all God's requirements are credited to you as a believer, to your account, and all your original sins, and all your actual sins, are transferred to the sacrificial Lamb, and God roasts the butchered Lamb under his wrath in your place. This is gained, as Christ preached, by repenting, and acknowledging this kingdom of God. It is an acknowledgement of the Christ and his work. Christ, by the mere good pleasure of his Father, was set apart and given as the Redeemer and Head of the church and offers salvation in repentance and submission to God's kingship. He was perfectly acquainted with the nature and extent of the work to which he was called in covenant with his Father, in order to accomplish everything needful for your salvation. He was completely willing and wholly determined to offer himself up as a sacrificial Lamb, to be slaughtered, butchered, killed, and chastised for you, his people, under the wrath of God. He did this to substitute himself in your place and acquire for you repentance, faith and eternal salvation.

Your heart, as I have said many times, should be soaked in the blood of Christ. How is man freed from misery of death and hell and saved? Enter the kingdom of the Savior by his work, and that condition is upon repentance, soaked in Christ's blood. To repent is to turn from your evil ways, to follow God's ways, being soaked in Christ's blood. This should be the grounds of eminent joy for you, being soaked in Christ's blood. Repentance is a soaking of your heart in the blood of Jesus; it is the substitutionary atonement of his work and merit applied to you. It *may be* you thought you were a good person, as you think most people are generally good. Jesus said that to enter the kingdom, to enter his kingdom, of which he is King, is to enter by the door of repentance, and this implies in it all his understanding of atonement, that you are bad, and have a bad record and a bad heart; that you need someone

Chapter 4: Christ's Substitutionary Atonement

else to save you. We call that ... a Savior, we call that name *Jesus*, the sweetest name for sinners. God is called by many names, but I think, none is more sweet than *Savior*. Maybe you thought you mostly do what is right, and are not so bad as others; but your heart in this is deceiving you if you do not take the road that Christ lays out in his substitution, and by his means. Bound in the shackles of death and hell in Adam's filth and original transgression which was credited to your account, you must hear this first sermon of the Christ summed up in the kingdom, and repent, and amend your ways and follow him by faith. This is why Christ is offered once for all, not time and time again. He can save you, and is the Savior. He does this as King, by God's kingdom rules.

And in this substitutionary atonement, he gives you a very special gift. It is a gift of *discrimination*. Repentance is that gift, for it is the foundation of salvation. Repentance makes a *discriminating line* for you. Either one repents or they don't. Either one is soaked under the blood of the Christ, or he isn't. Either one is saved or lost. Either one is a sheep or a goat, one does not become another; a sheep does not become a goat. There is no parable of the lost goats. They are lost sheep that are found by extravagant love in the work of the Shepherd who risks all to save that one sheep. Either one is a repenting sheep or a rebel goat.

You must know this substitutionary atonement, according to Christ's doctrine, if you are to be converted and saved. It is a great privilege to turn to God, because turning to him is based on a foundation of grace, Heb. 6:1, "Not laying again the foundation of repentance." The building of Christ's substitutionary atonement is once laid, and repentance is once laid down by grace. It is never done away with, but rather, laid once, just like the foundation of a building. One does not do away with the foundation of the building after its built. The building has a foundation in Christ, and the manner to enter his kingdom is through his atonement, by *repenting in light of it.*

All your believing, all your looking to Jesus, all your heeding and watching and such is all set on the foundation of all religion, which is built on the foundation of the substitutionary atonement of the Christ, and found in the kingdom by repentance. It is the great highway to enter into the kingdom, and it is set squarely on the work of Christ's substitutionary atonement, that it alone may usher you into the kingdom. This is the substance of *all* Christ's preaching.

In the next chapter we will consider the reign of the King in the church in his word and sacraments.

Chapter 5:
God Reigns as King Over His Church in the Word and Sacraments

"From that time Jesus began to preach, and to say, Repent: for the kingdom of heaven is at hand," (Matt. 4:17).

We have considered the kingdom, the King, repentance before his holy throne, and also the atonement of the Christ as substitutionary, all summed up in Christ's "short hand" words in Matthew 4:17. Then, to receive this kingdom, to receive this King, to enter into the kingdom by repentance, is to then partake of all the benefits of the Great King and his work. This is particular to his church, and this particular oversight of the King and his kingdom extends to all its benefits. *One* of these benefits is the manner in which Christ rules over his people through the Word of God. God rules his church *by his word*. A visible representation of the word is the Lord's Supper. It demonstrates a number of pictures and truths attested to by the word of God. I will only give you, in this chapter, a very basic and practical idea about this supper in light of the word and the benefits from it. You may think, this chapter is out of place. I can assure you that it is not, and it is particular to our aim and study. Let's consider that in the following way.

How does the *kingdom* suddenly include in it this aspect of the Lord's Supper? Why speak about the Supper as part of the kingdom; there are so many "things" (spiritual benefits) to choose from?

When the church is assembled together, and they sit down at Christ's table, it is a pledge of their sitting down with Abraham, Isaac, and Jacob, and drinking of the new wine in their Father's kingdom, (Matt. 26:29). When Christ instituted the Lord's Supper, he spoke to his disciples *of a kingdom*, Luke 22:30, "That ye may eat and drink at my table in my kingdom." His kingdom and dominion are forever established *which the supper demonstrates*. It is a kingdom that cannot be moved, purchased by the blood of the King, which should raise the affections of his subjects to heaven and heavenly things which the Supper points to. Why? That his people may be more *confirmed* in the blessed hope of the kingdom's establishment, and future prosperity. It is at this table they come to taste of the cup of blessing which Christ has prepared for them in his own blood. Meals in general have a prominent place in the gospels, especially in the gospel of Luke. There was the great feast in the house of Levi (Luke 5:29), and the dinner with Simon the Pharisee (Luke 7:36–50). There was the master returning from the wedding banquet (Luke 12:35–38), and the parable of the great banquet (Luke 14:15–24) through to the meal with the men on the way to Emmaus (Luke 24:28–35). But the most important banquet in the gospels is the Lord's Supper because it is the meal *of the kingdom*, a feast of the love of the Savior and covenant renewal.

Christ's particular reign as King is over his church through his atonement, is seen in the power of the Word of God as represented in the Lord's Supper. There are many blessings by the *word* to the church. But tied to the atonement, in God's rule and reign by his Spirit, is this *kingdom feast*.

First consider that the Supper itself is the King's prerogative to issue because he is Lord of his church. The Supper fulfills the Passover because Christ is now our Passover (1 Cor. 5:7). Christ commands Christians to be baptized, and to observe the Lord's Supper, that his kingdom may in this way be distinguished from the synagogue of Satan (Rev. 2:9, 3:9), which distinction he makes for his own glory, and for the comfort and salvation of his disciples.

In Christ's kingdom are a great many spiritual benefits that are bestowed for their holy good (Eph. 1:3). In particular, this is especially true of the sacrament of the Lord's Supper since it holds in it, certain themes that are directly related to the kingdom, and the atonement of Jesus who came preaching the kingdom by way of repentance. It is not that *walking in the Spirit* is not important. It is not that *casting off sin* is not important. It is not that considering the preached word is not important, or the meaning behind baptism. These themes I have covered extensively in other places.[1] So we turn our attention to an important part of the Christian walk, which is to consider the Lord's *kingdom feast.*

Christ's reign is seen in the sacrament of the Lord's Supper. The sacrament of the Lord's Supper houses in it the themes of the expiatory death of Christ for sinners, and an eschatological, an end times theme, in relation to the coming of the kingdom in its fullness.[2] It houses a remembrance to the work and merit of the Christ; for he has prepared and furnished a table for the provision of his family. Children are often delighted for their parent's work in preparing them their meals, especially when their favorite dishes are served. Like children to their favorite meals, so the Christian looks to Christ's supper as a feast and a delight. It houses a hope in new wine which will be ultimately drunk with Christ when all his family are untied together in his Father's kingdom (Matt. 26:29).

The new feature in this supper is that Jesus' body will be the food and his blood the drink of his disciples for *right now* his *kingdom is upon you*. The Lord's Supper is what Paul says, "the preaching of the Lord's *death* till he come," (1 Cor. 11:26); it contains *all* of the

---

[1] See my works: *Walking Victoriously in the Power of the Spirit*, *Joseph's Resolve: Or the Unreasonableness of Sinning Against God*, and my works in the 5 Marks series.
[2] It is a visual aid that Christ gave his people of the substitutionary atonement of his work and merit in his death.

gospel. It is a kingdom proclamation about the, "who, what, why and how," of the gospel. It is a festive banquet about God, his being, and his works. Banquet imagery is prominent in both Testaments with reference to the kingdom of God. Isaiah foresaw the judgment of the nations and the deliverance of Israel followed by the Lord's reign over his people (Isa. 24:23); the inauguration of that reign is accompanied by a huge banquet to which all peoples are invited (Isa. 25:6-8; *cf.* Luke 13:29). Meals which were shared following the sacrifice of animals in the Old Testament prefigure that great feast when there will be no more death, tears, or reproach for the people of God (Isa. 25:7; *cf.* Rev. 21:4). This meal follows Christ's death; the fulfillment of all types. The banquet of the New Covenant directs attention to the past, present and future; especially in hope when the redeemed will drink fine wine (Isa. 25:6) with Christ in the kingdom of God (Luke 22:14–20). Are these not Christ's words? "I will not drink of the fruit of the vine, until the kingdom of God shall come," (Luke 22:18). In the witness of the first three gospels one finds the proclamation of the kingdom of God was Christ's predominant message. Matthew summarizes Christ's ministry with the words, "And he went about all Galilee, teaching in their synagogues and preaching the gospel of the kingdom," (Matt. 4:23). The Sermon on the Mount is concerned with the righteousness that qualifies men to enter the kingdom of God, (Matt. 5:20). The collection of parables in Mark 4 and Matthew 13 illustrate the "mystery" of the kingdom of God (Matt. 13:11; Mark 4:11). The establishment of the Lord's Supper looks forward to the establishing of the kingdom of God, it was what Christ longed for, to eat with his disciples, with an eye to the future. "Verily I say unto you, I will drink no more of the fruit of the vine, until that day that I drink it new in the kingdom of God," (Mark 14:25). By participating in the Lord's Supper (having *enhanced communion* with the King by a special means), all Christians anticipate that great final feast.[3]

Jesus is showing his disciples that his death satisfies God as a substitutionary atonement, and is the cause and the foundation of the salvation he had proclaimed to them as the gospel of the kingdom. This good news is the fulfillment of the New Covenant promised by the prophets which he now becomes its Testator. Moses was the testator of the oldness of the covenant, but Jesus is the Testator of the newness of the covenant; its *refreshment*. Moses' scaffolding around the building of the gospel is now no longer needed; the building is built. The scaffolding is taken away in types and shadows. Jesus' foundation and capstone forever stand perfected in building a spiritual building and ushering in the kingdom of God. Jesus gave his disciples bread and wine as his body and blood for

---

[3] I like the *language* that Walter Elwell uses when he says this is to "anticipate the final feast" in *Tyndale Bible Dictionary*, Tyndale Reference Library (Wheaton, IL: Tyndale House Publishers, 2001), 144.

them to eat and to drink as a new way of seeing this Testator's rule in his church by his death, but also by his resurrection, because such work provides *abundant* life. Jesus is not the *dead* Savior, he is the *risen* Savior, knowing that such would occur, rising on the third day; raising up that temple of his body and blood. In the ark of the testimony was a sign of resurrection in the budding dead rod of Aaron, the governing of God to his people in tablets of stone, and the bread which comes from heaven, a type of the Bread of Life which feeds God's people forever. All of these were housed...where? They were set under the mercy seat and the blood of sprinkling; all of them were under the atonement, where God draws close to his people in the *ark* of safety. Now, Jesus gives and commands his disciples to observe and maintain this sacrament, this great mystery. They had a sacrament of entrance into the church, which is baptism, and now they have a sacrament of remembrance, which is continual in a feast. "Do this in remembrance of me," (Luke 22:19). It makes the Lord's Supper into the meal of the covenant, the feast of the church, that Christ gathers together for himself as bride, those called out of the world.

It is a *redemptive* meal, a meal of rejoicing and joy because of the Lord's death which satisfied God's wrath against sin and takes away the infinite penalty associated with eternal death. He is not merely the one who dies on the cross, but bound up in preaching the crucified Messiah, is the *whole plan* of the kingdom *implied* which includes sitting down and banqueting with the King. Why do we not hear more about this in Christ's churches?

The Supper implies in it: Christ returned from this terrible death, because he is not only the crucified but also the *risen* Lord. He is the benefactor of the meal (Psalm 23:5). He remains as the host of the meal in his ruling and reigning as the great King in heaven over his people. He is *the* food and drink of eternal life for hungry and thirsty souls. This is why the bread is the bread of salvation, the bread of life, who has come down from heaven to work his covenantal work, and the cup is the "cup of redemption," the cup of salvation (blessing) in his blood (John 6:48; 1 Cor. 10:16). In covenant renewal, Christians long to be fed by the King and will be submissive to his will for them; they submit their whole lives to him in it. This is not merely "a hope," but that which is realized in the Messiah and his kingdom, and confirmed by Jesus Christ in his work, death, resurrection, ascension and present intercession with an eye to his final exaltation. It is by no means a *simple* meal, but the Lord's Supper is a *feast* to celebrate the New Covenant in Christ Jesus, a feast that is linked to the Passover fulfillment in the substitutionary atonement, and a hope towards the coming of the full kingdom of God; something *special* happens in it when Christians by faith partake of it. The Lord's Supper celebrates the realization of the New Covenant, but goes further as an anticipatory meal, predating the wedding feast of Rev. 19:9, "Blessed are they which are called unto the marriage supper of the Lamb."

The supper is a sign and seal, as much as it is a symbol of current reality, as much as it is an anticipatory act of what will come, as a means of grace. Everything in the supper as it pertains to the kingdom and its fulfilling reality is set squarely on Jesus Christ as the Great King who dispenses grace to his people, and who is the host of this banquet. He has authority, power and the means to dispense grace to his people in it *now*, and later for eternity at its fulfillment in the Kingdom of his Father. But he promises to dispense this grace as believers come together to partake of the new covenant meal as one body at the banquet of his feast, in which Christ himself is the banquet with all its blessings.

What *is* this sacrament? A sacrament is an outward visible sign of an inward and invisible grace. "That the Lord Jesus, the same night in which he was betrayed, took bread: And when he had given thanks, he brake it, and said, Take eat; this is my body, which is broken for you: this do in remembrance of me," (1 Cor. 11:23b-24). It comprises his word (which is his promise) and the visible representation of that word in these sacraments (which are a feeding exercise of grace on him). Christ has not instituted this sacrament in his church to merely touch, feel and see things; it is not carnal. The person who eats bread and drinks wine in a religious ceremony at church has *missed* the Supper altogether. Christ as King would have his people *draw virtue* from himself, all the graces which this sign represents. It is an outward visible sign of an inward *reality* which the Spirit will increase in all believers as they partake. It is like eating a sermon given from Christ himself in visible form with instantaneous enlightening at the moment one hears it; "And when the multitude heard this, they were astonished at his doctrine," (Matt. 22:33). "And they were astonished at his doctrine: for his word was with power," (Luke 4:32). These are not mere words, and they are never mere words, never a mere supper, something more, something *astonishing*.

As King, Christ would have his people come sit at his table, and attend it to receive his benefits. To him belongs the power to ordain sacraments in his church because he fulfilled the sacraments of the law. When Christ came, the Passover ceased because he is the church's Passover—that is—the Lamb by whose blood they are saved, (John 1:29), the *substitution*.

When Christ came, circumcision ceased because *he* is their circumcision, the Purifier and Cleanser of their sins, (Rev. 7:14), and Renewer of their heart. The Lamb is Christ on whom all feed and receive this sacrament with an assured faith that Christ died to give them life *in particular* and they *gain* more of his virtue in participating in it. The breaking of the bread signifies the wounding of his body. The pouring of the wine signifies the shedding of his blood. The eating of the bread and drinking of the wine signify that his flesh and blood nourishes in them eternal life.

Jesus took bread, "And when he had given thanks, he brake it, and said, Take eat." He would not eat it or break it before he had given thanks to God. People today eat common meals as if they were like a pig or dog, without ever giving thanks; they are animals when they eat. Christ shows his people what they must do when they eat, to give thanks, and when they partake. "In everything give thanks," (1 Thess. 5:18). When he had given thanks to God, then it was sanctified, blessed, and lawful to eat. So when Christians serve God in even menial tasks of eating and drinking, then it is lawful for them to use God's blessings, then they may eat and drink as Christ did, when they have given him thanks. And yet, this thanks in the Supper is far different, for the supper is far different. You'll hear ministers say that the Supper is *just* a time of remembrance. They've missed it completely. Jesus says, "This is my body." Luther was accompanied by Melancthon and Zwingli by Oecolampadius when they met together to discuss the Supper. Luther could not give up *hoc est corpus meum*, "this is my body," and wrote it in chalk on the table itself; for he believed there is something *different* going on in the sacrament than many ministers will tell you. Here is the fruit of Christ's thanks. He prayed that the bread and wine might be blessed in a special manner. Before, it was merely bread, but now with Christ's blessing attached to it, it becomes more; and the same with the wine. His kingly virtue has now attached *spiritual virtue* to it, that it does not only represent his body, but conveys his body and himself to his people.

The mystical resemblance is that the elements unite Christ to his people that they make suck virtue out of the King and his kingdom which is *upon them* in the act. He *blessed* the bread to make it a spiritual food. Then he *gave* the bread when he had broken it, so Christ by a lively faith communicates his body after he has crucified it, (Eph. 3:17) to his people, and now they eat of it. When the minister takes the bread to feed the people, they are to consider that King Jesus being God from everlasting took their flesh to save them. He is God with them, Immanuel near to them, broken for them; the Savior.

Paul wrote, "After the same manner also he took the cup, when he had supped, saying, This cup is the new testament in my blood: this do ye, as oft as ye drink it, in remembrance of me. For as often as ye eat this bread, and drink this cup, ye do show the Lord's death till he come. Wherefore whosoever shall eat this bread, and drink this cup of the Lord, unworthily, shall be guilty of the body and blood of the Lord. But let a man examine himself, and so let him eat of that bread, and drink of that cup," (1 Cor. 11:25-28). Also, "he took the cup...saying...For this is my blood of the New Testament," (Matt. 26:27-28), and "he said unto them, This is my blood of the new testament," (Mark 14:24).

Here is the promise of the Testator to the covenant, which this word *testament* shows forth a promise. It teaches that the sacrament confirms, strengthens, and nourishes faith because it seals the promise which Christians believe; in a special way that other means do not. The Supper is a witness to the New Testament to the New Testator of the Covenant of Grace. Christ called love a new commandment, (John 13:34), because he renewed it, so he calls the promise of salvation a New Testament because he renews it. Because as it was renewed to Seth, and after renewed to Abraham, and after renewed to David, so now he renewed it again, which should always be new and fresh to his people; refreshed, and renewed; covenant renewal. Every testament is confirmed with blood; the Old Testament was confirmed by the blood of goats, bullocks, and rams which could not save, (Heb. 9:18), but the New Testament is confirmed by the blood of Christ; his blood makes all that the Old Testament did to be acceptable before God; there was moral virtue in *his* work, and in nothing else. Which is why Christ says, "For this is my blood of the new testament," (Matt. 26:28). Christ says, "This cup is the new testament in my blood," (Luke 22:20).

The cup is the kingdom come, a *New Testament*, where the wine is his blood. For Christ says, "This cup is the new testament," as well as he says, "This bread is my body...this cup is my blood," (Matt. 26:26-28). This new cup fulfills the promises of the Old Testament

(Heb. 8:13). There are no more sacrifices and no more ceremonies, for now, all is by Spirit and truth, by the word, by God's command, without the ceremonies of old. Was it a special day when people went to see the animal sacrifice at the temple differing than at other days? Is it a special supper when Christians partake of the sacrament than other suppers? This *new testament* of this new Testator, is called a "testament in blood" where Christ confirmed his testament by his death; the King laid down his life for his people. "For the life of the flesh is in the blood," (Lev. 17:11), so the blood of Christ is the life of this testament. "Without the shedding of blood there is no remission of sins," (Heb. 9:22). The Supper in this way is diametrically opposed to all those who would deny Christ's substitutionary atonement, and casts them far from the kingdom and the meaning behind the Supper. The testament or covenant of the remission of sins is called *the New Testament in blood*; the blood of Christ is the seal of the *testament*, which shows remission of sins, and the sacraments are a seal of that blood, to witness that it was shed, to stand in it, to believe it, for his people *to suck virtue from it*. At the fall, the Covenant of Grace was set down, and it was cloaked with all kinds of shadows and types of something better to be revealed. Moses gave witness to those types and shadows as an *old* testator. But Christ is the *new* Testator, in fact the fulfillment of all those shadows. This is why his people drink at the prepared table which contain his body and blood; they do not merely view the blood on the doorposts of their house, but they ingest spiritual nourishment by faith; and yet, so many are just eating crackers and wine.

The fruit of this kingdom sacrament is in these words, "which is broken for you," (1 Cor. 11:24), that is, "which is shed for many for the remission of sins," (Matt. 26:28), which is the substitutionary atonement of the Christ. When the kingdom is *come upon you*, everything that Christ did, which he spoke, he did and spoke for his people, (2 Cor. 4:15), for their good. All which he suffered, he suffered for them, that the sins of men might be forgiven. Silver tongued Henry Smith said, "Christ's hand takes God's hand and man's hand and joins them together, and then the remission of sins is sealed. This is the will and testament of Christ."[4] How? The explanation is given, "For as often as ye eat this bread, and drink this cup, ye do show the Lord's death till he come," (1 Cor. 11:26). Christians eat the symbolic bread and drink this symbolic cup. They show the Lord's death, show forth this representation of his death. They are to do this until he comes in the end, when the final coming of the kingdom is completed. They have the "now" of the *testating* (witnessing) of the Christ occurring while they partake of the Supper, but there is a *not yet* to it as well. There

---

[4] Smith, Henry, *A Treatise on the Lord's Supper*, (Coconut Creek, FL: Puritan Publications, 2013) eBook, section on The Fruit of the Sacrament.

will be a day when the *not yet* will fulfill all things in heaven.

The Supper is solemn, though, in that, "Wherefore whosoever shall eat this bread, and drink this cup of the Lord, unworthily, shall be guilty of the body and blood of the Lord," (1 Cor. 11:27). Paul says, "For he that eateth and drinketh unworthily...not discerning the Lord's body," (1 Cor. 11:29). Whoever does not *make a difference* between this bread and common bread is accursed; they must make a difference between this covenant Supper and common suppers. Whoever says, "nothing is happening here, nothing special, nothing grand, there is no grace to be had," is accursed. Christ says, "My sheep hear my voice, and I know them, and they follow me," (John 10:27), where as Christians discern Christ's words, so they discern Christ's body; and therefore, as often as they come to the Lord's Table, they come into the Lord's presence with fear and trembling. They come sit at his table to eat his prepared meal. They come sit at his table to eat and drink the body and blood of Christ's work.

All those that receive this sacrament unworthily are *guilty* of his body and blood, as much as Judas or Pilate were. The word of God preached is the savor of death to them which receive it unworthily. They are traitors to the kingdom and to the Great King. This is why it follows, "But let a man examine himself, and so let him eat of that bread, and drink of that cup," (1 Cor. 11:28). Why are they traitors? They do not suck out the virtue of Christ's blood, but instead tread upon it by atheistical unbelief, by not *discerning* what is occurring in it. "And he saith unto him, Friend, how camest thou in hither not having a wedding garment? *(make note here)* And he was speechless. Then said the king to the servants, Bind him hand and foot, and take him away, and cast him into outer darkness; there shall be weeping and gnashing of teeth. For many are called, but few are chosen," (Matt. 22:12-14).

The virtues of the kingdom in the Supper are many. Christ comes and fulfills all that the kingdom shall offer, and does he not by his blood offer not merely a gift, but a whole kingdom? It is no small thing. Is the offering of his body and blood a small thing? It is the offering of the infinite sacrifice of Christ against sin, and it is the infinite power of Christ to work righteousness to appease the wrath of the Father. So, it is no small thing. He delivers to partakers a kingdom by his body and blood; it is by death and resurrected life that he does so. In fact, Scripture often equates both together when it is said that by his blood men are saved. It is by all his work, all his merit, all his suffering, his humiliation, his exaltation, that they are saved. It is a summary of the kingdom and its coming in that way. What do his body and blood do? Or, what ought to be thought about in the Supper in this way of the kingdom coming?

Christ's body and blood reconciles a whole body of believers together as his bride. It is the body and blood of a substitutionary atonement. It is a sacrifice of propitiation, 1 John 2:2 says, "And he is the propitiation for our sins: and not for ours only, but also for the sins of the whole world," which shows men are brought into favor with God by Christ's work and merit; he seats them at his table by satisfying God's wrath against them.

When Christ died, the veil of the temple was torn (Matt. 27:51), and this demonstrates that through Christ's blood the veil of a believer's sins is torn in two which interfered with the relationship between God and them. This is because Christ's body and blood are regenerating. "Whoso eateth my flesh, and drinketh my blood, hath eternal life," (John 6:54). It both produces life by the Spirit's work of applying it and prevents the second death which has no more sting for in Christ all is life, for even though one even dies, he yet lives.

Christ's body and blood are cleansing. "How much more shall the blood of Christ purge your conscience!" (Hebrews 9:14). By Christ's virtue, they are purifying. Thomas Watson said, "It is the King of heaven's bath. It is a laver to wash in. It washes a crimson sinner milk white. "The blood of Jesus cleanseth us from all our sin," (1 John 1:7)."[5]

Christ's body and blood pacifies the conscience and brings it peace. Man's conscience, "is naturally defiled," (Titus 1:15). Such defilement must be taken off.

---

[5] Watson, Thomas, *The Holy Eucharist*, (Coconut Creek, FL: Puritan Publications, 2012) eBook, section 2.

The means to affect it is the blood of Christ. By his body and blood, Christians have their "hearts sprinkled from an evil conscience," (Hebrews 10:22). This is the only way to have "consciences purged from dead works to serve the living God," (Hebrews 9:14), they must be reminded of this, in fact, they must *feast* on the idea.

It is done by the Spirit of Christ, "I will sprinkle clean water upon you, and ye shall be clean from all your filthiness," (Ezekiel 36:25). Christ's blood and Christ's Spirit, will cleanse the most foul sinner and the most defiled conscience. "But ye are washed, but ye are sanctified, but ye are justified, in the name of the Lord Jesus, and by the Spirit of our God," (1 Corinthians 6:11). This is the "refiner's fire and fuller's soap," (Malachi 3:2), this is that hyssop which will, "make us as white as snow," (Psalm 51:7), yes *more white* than snow. They are exercised in the promises of God, by repentance, and through faith. Repent for the kingdom is at hand, and now that the kingdom is on you, and now that it is in you and you in it, so be reminded of all that has occurred, and sit at my table and eat my body and drink my blood, he says, suck more virtue from my work. Christ says, "Now are ye clean through the word that I have spoken unto you," (John 15:3). That is to say, "the word accompanied with the power of my Spirit," for his disciples must be ready to take this supper, and must be his true disciples to eat it. Repentance is the way of cleansing. "Wash ye, make you clean, put away the evil of your doings from before mine eyes, cease to do evil, learn to do well," (Isaiah 1:16) and then, "though your sins be as scarlet, they shall be as white as snow," (Isaiah 1:18). Have faith which is of a cleansing nature. It will, "purge the heart and cleanse the conversation," (Acts 15:9). All this is attached to the King's feast. There is no supper without the kingdom. There is no kingdom without the King. There is no King in relation to the supper without his body and blood in atonement. There is no virtue in the Supper without them. There is no partaking of it rightly without a growing faith and a consideration of such things.

Christ's blood in this way, distributes the virtues of the kingdom to those who partake with a clean conscience. It causes men to come near to God, even boldly before the King's throne. "Having boldness therefore to enter into the holiest by the blood of Jesus," (Hebrews 10:19). Christ's body and blood are the keys which opens the kingdom for sinners to come before the great King, and to sit at his table.

If King Jesus offers such kingdom virtues by his body and blood in the mystery of the sacrament, with what solemn preparation, then, are Christians commanded to in order to partake of it, and reap its most sweet benefits? "Prepare your hearts unto the Lord," (1 Samuel 7:3). "Whosoever shall eat this bread and drink this cup of the Lord unworthily, shall be guilty of the body and blood of the Lord," (1 Corinthians 11:27). Examination is not merely done for personal help, but for the health of the whole body in the church. For everyone's benefit, not merely selfish reasons, examination is *commanded*, because people come to the table as a body, not bodily parts. Thomas Manton said, "There we groan and long in the Lord's Supper for new wine in our Father's kingdom, to put a heavenly relish upon our hearts."[6] This is why Jesus said, "Repent, for the kingdom of heaven is upon you," and he says it every time one partakes of anything they eat at his table, or anything they hear in his word; for his church is to come for grace in that place.

What must you do to draw virtue from the King in his Supper? Labor to get your faith (your heart of the new man) confirmed and strengthened, not neglecting any means that Christ has appointed for strength in the kingdom, for among such strengthening benefits is the very sacrament of the Lord's Supper. It is a chief and principal benefit of the King, and the feast of the kingdom if you understand it. The Lord's Supper instituted by Christ conforms you to the union you have and communion you share with Jesus to further grow up in him as one attached to the life-giving vine. It should be your care to maintain this blessed union and communion with Jesus Christ to the end that we do not neglect any means appointed for kingdom living. And there is no more proper ordinance in Christ's kingdom than that which so readily demonstrates and shows forth the body and blood of the King given for

---

[6] Manton, Thomas, *The Complete Works of Thomas Manton*, Volume 12 (London: James Nisbet & Co., 1873), 455.

his servants, that they may suck virtue from him by faith in this feast, than by the word of God, and this sacrament is a visible manifestation of that word. It is, sadly, an ordinance that is greatly slighted and neglected by too many professing Christians in the world. "Eat some bread, drink some wine," they think. What do you think of it? It is a mysterious sacrament instituted by Jesus Christ for confirming and assuring you of abiding in him, and his kingdom abiding in you; is it a table to eat to receive grace, to drink to receive grace? How are you, then, to partake of the Supper acceptably with reverence and godly fear? Each week how do you benefit from it?[7] You must benefit, [1] before the supper, [2] during the supper, and, [3] after the supper.

How do you benefit before the Supper? Self-examination is a reflexive act born out of being regenerate. In order to examine yourself, to see what must be done in order to have a good conscience in coming to the King's feast, and gaining the virtues of the Supper, certain qualities are exercised. There is a willingness to please God. To please him in all things. To please him always. To do all this truly, sincerely, and honestly. For, if we do not examine ourselves, we are at a loss about our spiritual state. We do not know whether we are interested in the covenant or whether we have a right to the seal of all its promises and

---

[7] I'm assuming your church partakes of the sacrament each week. Many churches do not do this to their spiritual detriment.

virtues, whether we are just eating crackers and wine; but know, such is never the case, for those who are eating crackers and wine are eating condemnation to themselves by mishandling the King's feast. This is why one must examine themselves. If a person comes to know the supper is next week, and they say, "I'm saved, and I know I'm a sinner, but I'm good with it." This is not what the Spirit means in examination – for consider:[8]

    Do you have a willingness to please God in all things at all times, truly, sincerely and honestly? If you have found that you personally own that gracious change in yourselves which was from the Spirit, you will find that your evil conscience has become a good conscience; you will know this because you regularly examine yourself in it. You think to yourself, "I was by nature as vile as the worst, as deeply guilty in Adam's sin as any; as terribly polluted with original sin as the worst reprobate, and had in me the seed of all sin, apt to be drawn to the foulest and grossest transgressions, and to "run to the same excess of riot with the worst," (1 Peter 4:4), yes, my very "soul and conscience was defiled," (Titus 1:15). You know well what that means. Have you thought that? But blessed be God that has made a covenant with me in the Savior Christ Jesus, and has given me a new spirit, given me a heart of flesh

---

[8] Much of the next paragraph is bound up in the words of Henry Tozer (1602-1650), *Attending the Lord's Table*, which is a wonderful treatise on the Supper with many practical outworkings to consider. It is published by Puritan Publications.

(Ezekiel 11:19), and has changed this defiled conscience into a pure conscience (Hebrews 9:14), a conscience both purified and pacified by the blood and Spirit of Christ (Colossians 1:20). Do you know that too? Your conscience cannot be cloaked in ungodly practices, nor in indifference (which is the plight of most Christians in this), nor in hypocrisy; all of that is opposite to the supper and defiles it.

    You will be affected, then, by God's visible word in the sacrament. So, you are affected by the promises of the gospel and God's loving big-heartedness and kindness to you, as well as all the precepts, threats, judgments, and mercies found all through the word. You will desire to readily yield to God's precepts. Whatever Christ commands, you do it with great attention, and you do it in joy and rejoicing. You do it quickly. *I made haste and delayed not to keep your commandments*, the Psalmist said. Josiah merely heard the book of the law read, and he immediately melts, rents his clothes, mourns and weeps (2 Kings 22:19), calls his people to covenant together for biblical reformation. You mourn under God's judgments, like the coronavirus, for your sins, and for others sins. Hezekiah felt God's rod on him and will "mourn like a dove, and chatter like a crane," (Isaiah 38:14). He was *moved* by the rod. How are you moved by God's rod? You love his staff; will you love his rod too? Are his rod and staff *both* comforts to you? And do you even know the difference? And do you not know he prepares a table for you in that sweet 23rd psalm? Let God strike Job with many afflictions in his decrees of trial regardless of all those secondary causes, and it will make him to sow "sackcloth upon his skin, and defile his horn in the dust," ... "it will make his face foul with weeping, and cause the shadow of death upon his eyelids," (Job 16:12, 15). Are you like Job, and do you feel that way? You are humbled under Christ's mercies if you love him and his kingdom. The more merciful that God is to you, the more tender you are for God. It is unavoidably reciprocal, for it is mutual.

Self-examination is a demanding reflexive act born out of being regenerate, given a new disposition and a new heart, a whole new kingdom indwells you. In order to examine yourself, to see what must be done in order to have a good conscience in coming to the King's feast each time, and gaining the virtues of the Supper, certain qualities are exercised. To live truly, sincerely, and honestly before him. This is why one must examine themselves. Therefore, "let a man examine himself, and so let him eat," (1 Cor. 11:28); that is, let him examine first and receive after. When we come to the Lord's Table, he would have our hearts upright. Is your heart upright?

Our doctrine is to be examined; our devotions are examined; our beliefs are examined; our life is examined, and all this by the instructions of the word from the mouth of the King of the kingdom we desire to have entrance into; this is what disciples do before coming to the table. Paul says, "Prove all things; hold fast that which is good," (1 Thess. 5:21). It is like proving gold in the fire, refining it; every time we partake, we consider, and we examine. Do you do this? Do you see why many churches do not practice the supper *weekly*, because *much work* is involved in self-examination.

What are we to examine? I give you four things to examine in light of the body and blood of Christ in saving you in order to draw virtue from the Supper.

[1] We examine our spiritual discernment. The gospel is hidden from the natural man, "The things of the Spirit of God are foolishness to him," (2 Corinthians 4:3). Are you naturally inclined or spiritually inclined? I know people for years, professing Christians, members of churches, who I can honestly say I have never heard them talk once about the sweetness of Christ, the work of Christ, the power of Christ's virtue. How can servants of the King never speak of him? The answer to that question is that they cannot, because they are natural men.

[2] We must examine what is our chief good. Worldly people are more concerned with this life than kingdom life, for they are not very concerned of the life to come, and not much of it enters their thoughts. Are you more concerned with this life, than the kingdom of heaven? How will you measure it? Let me give you an example of what I mean, measure yourself in this, examine yourself against this fellow:

Charles Bridgemen had no sooner learned to speak, than he took himself to prayer. He would learn the bible thoroughly, and would be sometimes teaching them their duty that looked after him. He was so religious, with savory words, his devotion so hearty, his fear of God so great, that many were ready to say, as they did of John, what manner of child shall this be? He would read the holy Scriptures much. He desired of more spiritual knowledge, and would be often asking very serious questions. He would not waste his time playing outside before he had poured out his soul to the Lord. He would not lie down in his bed until he has been on his knees. He would rebuke his brothers and sisters if they were at any time too hasty at their meals to eat without asking a blessing. Yet, he took on a lingering sickness and said of this life, "What are possessions and this life? I had rather have the kingdom of heaven than a thousand such inheritances." When he was sick he seemed taken up much with heaven, and asked very serious questions about the nature of his soul. He inquired how his soul might be saved? The answer was made about the applying of Christ's merits by faith. He was pleased with the answer, and was ready to give anyone that should desire it an account of his hope. Being asked whether he had rather live or die, he answered, "I desire to die, that I may go to my Savior." "If I had lived in the times of martyrs," said the child, "I would have run through the fire to have gone to Christ." When he died, the last words which he spoke were exactly these, "Pray, pray, pray, no, and yet pray more; and the more prayers the better, all prayer prospers; God is the best physician; into thy hands I commend my spirit. O Lord Jesus receive my soul? Now close my eyes; forgive me, father, mother, brother, sister, all the world! Now I am well, my pain is almost gone, my joy is at hand; Lord have mercy upon me, O Lord, receive my soul unto thee!" And in this way he yielded up his spirit to the Lord, when he was about twelve years old.

You see, Christians *choose the Lord for their portion and resolve to love him for his great love to them.* They cannot help but to speak about him, they are enraptured with him; it is their *life.* "Thou art my portion O Lord, I have said that I would keep thy Word," (Psalm 119:57). He is their portion, how can they not have such joy in him?

[3] We must examine whether our heart-sins are abhorrent and reviled and detested by us. You are to take very special notice of these, and consider what your position on them is. They are sins that continue to plague you; you know them intimately because you

anatomize them constantly in desiring to overcome them. David proves his uprightness by this statement, "I was also upright before thee and I kept myself from mine iniquity," (Psalm 18:23); do you keep yourself from your iniquity? Nathaniel Vincent said, "If Herod will keep his Herodias still against the admonition of John the Baptist, it plainly argues that he is void of grace, though he hears gladly and in part practices the word he hears."[9] Are we grieved at all our defects and sins, and desirous to have everything inappropriate corrected and remedied?

[4] We must examine whether we seek the kingdom of Christ and his righteousness before all other things. "We look not at the things that are seen, but at the things which are not seen. For the things that are seen, are temporal; but the things which are not seen are eternal," (2 Corinthians 4:18). Be like little Charles that could not go outside to play before he was on his knees in prayer. Before we partake of the feast of the supper we must search out and examine such things.

During the Supper we should be in examination. We call this *a seasonable meditation*. Our meditation should be threefold: Right before we partake. In the time of the consecration (the prayer) of the elements, then in the time of receiving.[10]

---

[9] Vincent, Nathaniel, *A Discourse on Self-Examination*, (Coconut Creek, FL: Puritan Publications, 2013) eBook, chapter 2.
[10] This was the *Westminster Assembly's* view, and can be found in many of their individual writings.

Before the consecration,[11] when the minister is going towards the table, meditate on these two things. 1. Seeing the table spread, and the elements set on it, we are to consider, what place we have come to; I say this every week, namely, the table of the great King of heaven and earth. We should carefully and reverently, behave ourselves, both in body and mind, laying aside all earthly thoughts no matter what they are. Exod. 3:5, "Put off thy shoes from off thy feet, for the place whereon thou standest, is holy ground." Because as the place is holy, so also God himself is there among us, as he says in Matthew 18:20, "Where two or three are gathered together in my name there am I in the midst of them." He is in the midst of us, seeing not only our outward gesture (what we do with our body during worship which people are often very careless about) but our very hearts and affections; he minds them all.

2. When we hear the minister say, this is the body and blood of Christ in the sacrament, we must consider that God by his minister freely invites us to his table if we are Christians. We are not worthy to come on our own, but the Lord is pleased in mercy to call you, and in humility and obedience you come. We ought joyfully and thankfully to meditate on the great love of God in setting apart his Son for our redemption. We were rebels, enemies, now made at peace with God. Such is represented in taking these elements, and

---

[11] These three points are stated by Henry Tozer in his work, *Attending the Lord's Table*, but I have enlarged them here.

setting them apart to be distributed to us, as seals and pledges of reconciliation. Joyfully in respect of the benefit, which by this comes to us, and thankfully in respect of God's love, which is greater than all the hearts of men joined in one are able to express.

When we see the bread broken and the wine poured out, we ought to be exercised in comfort as much as we are in fear. Considering that the bread is broken and the wine poured out to represent to us the crucifying of Christ's body, and the shedding of his blood for our sins. Christ Jesus was broken on the cross, and suffered an accursed death for us; by whose merits, we trust, that we shall escape the curse of that death which is due for our sins. We should have an element of sorrow, and that for our sins; the grievousness of which was such that they could not be satisfied for, without the precious blood of Christ Jesus. When we see the bread broken etc., we should think: How vile am I, that by my sins I should in this way wound my merciful and loving Redeemer.

After the prayer of consecration we should consider the sweetness of Jesus, humbly acknowledging that we can come and eat and dwell with him, and that he gives us such a kingdom as this. You should think, Christ, with the benefits of his death, comes to sanctify and comfort my sinful soul, in full assurance of which I am now to receive these signs and seals. Lift up your soul in faith in this. Trust that Christ will come to you. Trust that he will minister to you, and he will.

While we eat the bread, everyone should ponder Christ's cross: That Christ was crucified on the cross for me in particular. That I now receive this bread broken, by which my body shall be nourished. That I have received spiritually his body crucified with all its benefits; the full pardon of all my sins; and the strengthening and refreshing of my sinful soul.

When we drink the wine, we should consider: I truly believe that his blood was shed for me. I have received this wine for the remission of my sins. My sins are fully washed away and my conscience purified. According to his promise, I shall never hunger nor thirst anymore; because with this bread and wine I have received his flesh, which is meat indeed, and his blood which is drink indeed. Increase in me a hearty love to God and the church, who have now participated with me, so that we may serve him as we ought, and that nothing may be able to separate us from his love.

After the Supper we should examine ourselves. What ought to be running through your mind after such an examination, to gain kingdom benefits and suck virtue from Christ? Think this way, Henry Tozer said, "The King has commanded me who have entered into his kingdom, and all believers, to eat of this broken bread together, and to drink of this cup together, in remembrance of his work and merit; adding these promises, first, that his body was offered and broken on

Chapter 5: God Reigns as King in the Lord's Supper

the cross for me, and his blood shed for me, as certainly as I see with my eyes the bread of the Lord broken for me, and the cup communicated to me: and further, that he feeds and nourishes my soul to everlasting life, with his crucified body and shed blood, as assuredly as I receive from the hands of the minister and taste with my mouth the bread and cup of the Lord, as certain signs of the body and blood of Christ the King."[12]

When the soul is enabled to live on Christ, to feed on Christ, that you feel your heart live on Christ, sucking and drawing virtue from Christ, mortifying your corruptions and quickening your heart in the way of holiness, this is a true evangelical life in which you participate in the kingdom of heaven that Christ preached as the Great King.

The King gave you this Supper as a help to your soul to remind you of all his work; to be mindful is to exercise the mind and warm the heart. If you do not take time to consider such things before partaking, while partaking and after partaking, you are eating crackers and drinking a sip of wine. What good will that do you? There is no magic in the elements. But join the elements of the King's Supper to a faithful examination and contemplation of the King's feast, and one truly begins to know what it means that he

---

[12] See Tozer's excellent work *Attending the Lord's Table* on these ideas. Though there are many works on the Supper, I wanted to keep this practical and simple, and only referred here to Henry Smith and Henry Tozer in a larger capacity than any of the other works that could be cited.

prepares a table for me in the presence of mine enemies ... my cup runneth over. Suck the virtue of Christ from the Supper by faith in such holy contemplations of the Christ's kingdom feast.

In the next chapter we will consider the practical dimension of the coming of the finality of the kingdom and the rule of the Christ in his exaltation.

Chapter 6:
God Reigns as King in His Final Coming and Exaltation

"From that time Jesus began to preach, and to say, Repent: for the kingdom of heaven is at hand," (Matt. 4:17).

By way of reminder, Jesus preached as God's Divine Messenger and Herald, the Exegete of the Father, to declare him. In his first sermon he preached the kingdom and repentance. To preach the kingdom involves the King and all his works. God is absolute King over the universe. He is particular as King in his government of the church. He rules over the fall, reigns as King, and can reverse the fall. He does this through covenant. He does this through his Mediator. He does this for his church in blessing it and preparing it to meet him at the wedding day as the Supper demonstrates. He does this through his one and only Christ, who is his Surety for sinners and a loving Savior.

To gain repentance, from the King, in his dominion over the fall, is to gain it by God's good pleasure, and by the substitutionary atonement of his Mediator, and its application of power by the Spirit sent from his exalted throne in heaven, the right hand of power in which he judges and makes war. Jesus will return to establish the finality of his Father's kingdom, and as the divine Warrior[1] he does so in conquest of all those that oppose his kingdom. This idea is a result of his divine kingship, in which Christ as the warrior King, who, in his return, his primary directive is the preservation of his people, and the final destruction of all his enemies. He preserves the peace and prosperity of a people through the act of warfare—the violence he strikes the kingdom of darkness by and establishes the kingdom of light.

All the covenant promises will come to pass which include the sovereign King to pursue and triumph over his Son's enemies. It is a holy war Christ wages, and in it, he is victorious. I do not wish to give you a full orbed view of the coming of Christ and his judgment; this would take many chapters, in fact, many

---

[1] Christ is the great Warrior King who will judge men for their sins. Nahum 1:2 states "God is jealous, and the LORD revengeth; the LORD revengeth, and is furious; the LORD will take vengeance on his adversaries, and he reserveth wrath for his enemies." This is an anthropomorphic expression *of hate* which can be seen in such Scriptures as Psalm 5:5, "The foolish shall not stand in your sight; You hate all workers of iniquity." Psalm 11:5 says the same, "The LORD tries the righteous: but the wicked and him that loves violence His soul hateth." Psalm 7:11-13 goes so far as to show that God even ordains the very arrows that He set to strike them dead, "...God is angry with the wicked every day. If he turn not, he will whet his sword; he hath bent his bow, and made it ready. He hath also prepared for him the instruments of death; he ordains his arrows against the persecutors." In a type of analogous "anthropomorphism," the Warrior King is readying himself to do battle with the wicked, not desiring their salvation. For the wicked, Christ whets his sword and readies his arrows. As Hosea 9:15 says, "All their wickedness is in Gilgal: for there I hated them."

books have been written on this.² I will only touch on some practical ideas that surround it as it fits in light of the kingdom and what we have studied in this way so far; so take this more as an exhortation of truths you may in fact even know, but ought to ponder and hide them in your heart for practical reasons that fuel your desire to serve him in your Christian walk.

Christ's reign as King over his church and the world is finalized in the last judgment when he shall come undoubtedly, personally, visibly, gloriously, terribly and very unexpectedly.³ There is a time that the Son of Man, the Great King will return and the consummation of the kingdom will be laid down. It will be final. There will be no undoing it. What does Jesus say about this finality of the coming of his kingdom? How does his kingdom come in its finality? What does he do? What will happen?

All through his kingdom parables Jesus speaks eschatologically, he speaks about the end times, and its relation to the kingdom. So one must ask, how and when will Christ Return? Let's briefly consider that he shall come certainly, personally, visibly, gloriously, terribly and very unexpectedly.

---

² See an excellent summary work on this topic by Christopher Love (1618-1651) called *Christ's Ascension and Second Coming from Heaven*. It is published by Puritan Publications.

³ Christopher Love makes this notation in his work in expanding these various adjectives. I only make mention of these for the purposes of setting the stage of this particular point of Christ's return in general.

His coming is without a doubt, set in God's decree from before the foundations of the world. It is certain, without *any* doubt, because as God is immutable, so is his will and his word. They shall come to pass. He will not have it any other way.

Christ's coming is personal, not sending another, but coming himself to finish his exalted work, 1 Thess. 4:16, "For the Lord himself shall descend with a shout from heaven," *etc.*

His coming shall be visible, Acts 1:11, "This same Jesus which is taken up from you into heaven shall so come in like manner, as ye have seen him go into heaven." Everyone shall see the glory of the King; no one will miss it, and he will not return secretly or invisibly, but visibly seen. The wicked shall see him to their shock and dread, and the godly shall see him to their joy and comfort.

His coming shall be glorious, Daniel 7:10, "A fiery stream issued, and came forth from before him, thousand thousands ministered unto him; and ten thousand times ten thousand stood before him, the judgement was set, and the books where opened." Matt. 24:30 says, "And they shall see the Son of man coming in the clouds of heaven, with power and great glory."

His coming will also be terrible for the wicked. Isaiah 13:9, "Behold the day of the Lord cometh, cruel both with wrath and fierce anger, to lay the land desolate, and he shall destroy the sinners thereof out of it." Rev. 6:17, "For the great day of his wrath is come, and who shall be able to stand?"

His coming, by his tarrying, shall be very unexpected and catch many unaware. "Therefore be ye also ready: for in such an hour as ye think not the Son of man cometh. Who then is a faithful and wise servant..." (Matt. 24:44-45).

The Great King, interestingly, does not tell the saints *when* he will return, and bring his salvation, and bring his reward, and bring all his final judgments on purpose. Why is this? They are to be persuaded that there shall be a day of judgment, yes, but in this Christ does two things. He deters men from sin in this, that they live well before he comes, so that when he comes, he will find faith. And he, for greater comfort to the godly in their adversity, where the day of their deliverance is not known, but promised to have benefits of comfort while in adversity. They must shake off all carnal security, and always be watchful, because they do not know at what hour the Lord will come and require an accounting; so, they are to take heed, and watch, and prepare always. They are to always be prepared to say, "Come, Lord Jesus, come quickly."

Christ never says, "now" doesn't count. It is quite the opposite in his kingdom. *Right now counts forever.* Right now counts in light of the coming of his kingdom in its fullness and finality. Consider, then, the tarrying of the One who is to arrive soon.

In Christ's parables, a number of them are important concerning the coming of the kingdom and the Great King, or the Bridegroom or the Master, or the nobleman. They all have "a sense of delay."[4] The parable of the unjust judge in Luke 18:1–8. Jesus teaches his disciples, "always to pray and not to faint." The unjust judge would not avenge the woman "for a while". It is unsure as to what time this might be, but it is not *instant*. There is a delay in justice for her, though in the end, the delay proves helpful to her character and she gets justice. The parables of the coming of the "Lord," or of the "bridegroom." Mark 13:33–37 shows the man taking a far journey. Matthew 24:42–51, compared with Luke 12:35–46 the watchful and faithful servant wait for the master to come. Matthew 25:1–13 explains the parable of the ten virgins with their oil, and their waiting for the Bridegroom to arrive. In all these parables the disciples are to be watchful and take heed and be very diligent as it regards the kingdom. The ten virgins, "while the bridegroom tarried" (*chronizontos*, Matt. 25:5), show there is a delay in the fullness of his coming. "Watch therefore, for ye know neither the day nor the hour wherein the Son of Man cometh," (Matt. 25:13). There is *delay*.

---

[4] The phrase "sense of delay" is an excellent use of the idea in M. H. Cressey's, "Time," ed. D. R. W. Wood et al., *New Bible Dictionary*, (Leicester, England; Downers Grove, IL: InterVarsity Press, 1996), 1187.

Chapter 6: God Reigns as King in His Final Coming

Is he not coming as, "the thief in the night" (Matt. 24:43; Luke 12:39)?[5] No one knows when the thief will strike. There is an anticipation, but no one knows when; preparations ought to be made in light of it "But of that day and hour knoweth no man, no, not the angels in heaven, neither the Son, but the Father" (Matt. 24:36; Mark 13:32). It is very secret. Everyone should be ready to give an account of their stewardship when the Master comes, and then calls them to account.

The parable of the pounds, Luke 19:11–27, we find the departure of the nobleman, and his command to his servants to be diligent in working for the kingdom because they do not know when he will return. "...that he might know how much every man had gained by trading," (Luke 19:15). He expected them to be up and doing, never idle; not only making the most of it, but being very fruitful in their positions.

The parable of the talents speaks of "a man travelling into a far country," (Matt. 25:14–30). He comes back and requires of them an answer to his gifts to them. What did they do? There is a delay, but there is also work to be done on behalf of the kingdom for those who have been allowed entrance into it. In fact, those who have the kingdom dwelling in them live and act in a certain light while the Master is away; and

---

[5] See Kenneth E. Bailey's, *Jesus through Middle Eastern Eyes: Cultural Studies in the Gospels*, (Downers Grove, IL: IVP Academic, 2008), 400ff, for a helpful understanding of this idea of a *thief* culturally.

those who do not really have the kingdom in them will fail at the task as the one who buried his talent and did nothing with it.

Why the delay, why not just consummate and finish the kingdom immediately? There are two reasons for delay. The first is to bring in the whole church. God is not slow in keeping his promises, as Peter tells us (2 Peter 3:9). A day is as a thousand years, and a thousand years as a day. He desires that not one of his children shall perish. But that all *his* people, his church, his bride, come to repentance, and they all will. God will see to it through his Christ.

Then, secondly, also, to bring in the maximum reward for those who are part of the kingdom in their diligence with what he has given them to do. So, he tarries to bring in the fullness of those that belong to the kingdom, and to bring the reward for those who have gained entrance into the kingdom. Christ returns in glory and his reward is with him ... for them.

We should make a note on *reward* and the coming of the kingdom by *degrees*; it is not instantaneous. God has appointed a day in which he will judge the world in righteousness by Jesus Christ, to whom all power and judgment are given of the Father. On this day, not only the apostate angels shall be judged, but also all people that have lived on earth, will appear before the tribunal of the Great King, to give an account of their thoughts, words, and deeds; and to receive according to what they have done in the body, whether good or evil. Do you know how replete the Scriptures are with language, filled as it were, with it?[6] Why is such said if it is all merely *by grace alone*? Why is there any judgment at all if God is so gracious? Again, this thrashes violently against the twisted Antinomian idea of "solitary grace."[7] Why not just saved and unsaved? Why not just leave it at sheep and goats and that's it? What is this *accounting* of men's lives do if God knows all things, if for the saints it makes no difference at all ... or does it? Why a waiting on the tarrying Master, to await a final judgment, why does Jesus speak so often this way, and describe his kingdom in that way? And what is to be done in the meantime? "Why are you idle here in the market all day long?" As much as we speak about the finality of Christ's coming, and its glorious certainty, there is an element of living that must be done beforehand. Christ is the supreme Judge of the world and the Great King who ushers in his kingdom, and at this final time, at the finality in the Great Judgment, all things are judged that have occurred based on what is done in the body. That is a very interesting thought to consider in all the judgment passages of Scripture. Things done, not just in the mind, but also in the now, the here, the body, the

---

[6] Acts 17:31; John 5:22, 27; 1 Cor. 6:3; 2 Peter 2:4; Jude 1:6; Eccl. 12:14; Matt. 12:36-37; Roman 2:16; 14:10, 12; 2 Cor 5:10.

[7] The idea that, "I don't need to do anything, because all I need is for Jesus to save me by grace. There are no works needed in my Christian life because Jesus is the one who saves me and brings me to heaven."

life, its stewardship or lack thereof; how people live and glorify God with their bodies, their mouths, their hands, their ears, their eyes, and such, will be judged by him. The body cannot do anything without the heart, soul and mind. This is why Jesus spoke this way (Mark 12:30); he often falls on one side or the other which must include the work of the whole person. There is a time coming when Christ will in the most public and solemn manner judge everyone from all of time at his coming for all they have done in their *personhood*. He will bring in Adam and Nimrod, and Pharaoh, Judas, and Thomas, Calvin and Servetus, Arminius and Ames, Burroughs and Hodges, and Edwards and Wesley, Finney and Graham, and you and me. All will be brought before the Great King seated on the throne, and they will give an account of everything done in the body, even down to what Christ calls, *idle words*. Such a judgment shall be done in light of the righteousness of Christ, the divine Son of Man, and his law. It will be according to his character, which is his law; how men today in the church despise his law, and throw it out, cast it out; they will be judged for casting it out, or how they upheld it, in every point. Men will either be saved by Christ and ushered into his kingdom in its fullness, or damned by him and cast away from the blessedness of the kingdom because of their relationship to the Savior, and his character. This will be final at the judgment when the books are opened. But what a blessed thing it is for the King to have told the subjects of his kingdom about it; he warned them about it; it is of no surprise to them.

Yet, this is not simply a black and white finality as it is considered in the gospels or the Old Testament or the letters of the apostles with those saved and lost. The preaching of the kingdom by John, by the Christ, the Apostles, all surround *action*; not just saved by grace and *done*; not just this one final point of things being, well, final. Disciples don't sit around now waiting for Christ to return. It is not merely a *theoretical* final coming and exaltation of the King. People, yes, are saved by Christ, assuredly by him alone; but something more occurs here as attached to kingdom principles and the coming of final judgment. It is why Christ set up *rewards*. In point of fact, rewards will be handed out based on their *works*, and punishment handed out for the lack thereof. The wicked have earned wages; earned damnation. It is not merely by original sin that they are damned. It is by the exercise of the aggravations of their sin, that they will receive recompense as it stands in relation to the laws of the lawgiver. "For the *wages* of sin is death;" (Rom. 6:23); what the wicked earn they will by degrees of sins, be compared to the righteous degree of the law. All their sins will condemn them at the final coming of the King who comes to judgment. Some will receive greater damnation than others (Mark 12:40), based on that righteous character of the King and his law, and some less. But all will give an account, undoubtedly, before his throne.

At the same time that saints are redeemed by the Christ equally, they all receive a denarius for their living wage, the degree of the joy and rejoicing of every saint saved by Christ is not the same when they go to heaven, they receive rewards too, like the wicked but in reverse. The same perfect obedience of Jesus Christ saves all men who are saved in the very same way to the same extent; everyone gets into heaven who are saved by the same blood, and the white robe of righteousness to its infinite merit. "Thou hast redeemed us to God by thy blood out of every kindred, and tongue, and people, and nation," (Rev. 5:9). What can the saints say to this, but, "What shall I render unto the LORD for all his benefits toward me?" (Psa. 116:12). They are all saved completely, and totally, by faith in Christ, regardless of the degree of grace in them; a burning fire of zeal, or a smoking wick (Isa. 42:3; Matthew 12:20). But at this final judgment, or tally of all their works, they will be rewarded too, and then enter heaven, to sit down with Abraham, Isaac and Jacob at the great feast (Matthew 8:11). Whether a powerful Paul, or a bruised reed, Christ covers them and they are accounted righteous by *his* works to be saved. But what of their works, what did they do while he tarried? Why is there a tribunal for the saints saved by grace to come before a tarrying Master? Why don't they just walk right into heaven, and why don't they all receive the same recompense of works if it is all *just by grace*? They have different *degrees* of joy and rejoicing based upon their works based on what they do while they wait here. Jonathan Edwards said, "It is his free and sovereign act that [the King] ... gives higher degrees of glory as a reward to the higher degrees of good works, not because they deserve it, but because it pleases him."[8] Christ has so setup his Father's gracious kingdom where good works will then increase happiness, the one who has had all manner of grace bestowed upon them, and will in fact, then, increase one's rewards. "But love ye your enemies, and do good, and lend, hoping for nothing again; *[why?]* and your reward shall be great," (Luke 6:35). What one does or does not do will be great or not. This argues *degrees* of reward. Some will have greater rewards, and everyone will *rejoice* that such rewards are given to others.

Now, in this life, men envy, and don't like that idea at all of works in this light; you remember the vineyard workers in Matthew 20. They don't want to be judged by their works, they just want to appease themselves by doing works that give them a good feeling about salvation or not. This is one of the reasons the wicked are so angry at the judgment. Job even said, "I know that my redeemer liveth" ... and "I am escaped with the skin of my teeth," (Job 19:20), as if he's just made it over the line into the kingdom. It is not easy to

---

[8] Edwards, Jonathan, "None Are Saved by Their Own Righteousness," in *Sermons and Discourses, 1723–1729*, ed. Harry S. Stout and Kenneth P. Minkema, vol. 14, The Works of Jonathan Edwards (New Haven; London: Yale University Press, 1997), 338.

enter into the kingdom, for God requires whole and immediate repentance for entry, but then all things count as it pertains to what one does *with the kingdom* that Christ has begun *in them* while awaiting their Master's final, return in judgment. Did Christ speak this way of reward for the righteous? Yes, he did this constantly. Sometimes people wonder why the church has in it Pelagians, and Semi-Pelagians, and Arminians? These people twist what Christ says, but they are often those who overbear in pressing the need to be *up and doing*, but to a sinful fault. They want to be up and doing to *earn their place in heaven*. It is no wonder that carnal men take such things and are in the church trying to work them out. Jesus says his people are to be up and doing *in light of their salvation* which he has so graciously bestowed so that their happiness will be great, and that they will have abundant life. So, it is not really a wonder that such deviant views exist in the church; the devil will always warp the truth for natural men to work in a wrong way. But many Christian people think abundant life is just once applied and done.

No, abundant living is the same as saying abundant life; to live. What is it *to live?* Right now counts forever because it is not known when the certain, visible, personal, glorious, terrible return of the Christ shall be. "For whosoever shall give you a cup of water to drink in my name, because ye belong to Christ, verily I say unto you, he shall not lose his reward," (Mark 9:41). "For the Son of man shall come in the glory of his Father with his angels; and then he shall reward every man according to his works," (Matt. 16:27). Rewards are according to his works? Yes, and lots of works, or a few works ... rewards will be given accordingly. "Wait, wait," you say, "I thought it was all of grace?" This reward has nothing to do with "getting into heaven," which is by grace, through faith alone, which is a gift of God, not by works lest any man should boast, and yet, for those saved by grace, *he's ordained works that we should walk in them,* (Eph. 2:8-10, see verse 10). And, "For the day of the LORD is near upon all the heathen: as thou hast done, it shall be done unto thee: thy reward shall return upon thine own head," (Oba. 1:15). And, "Behold, the LORD hath proclaimed unto the end of the world, Say ye to the daughter of Zion, Behold, thy salvation cometh; behold, his reward is with him, ..." (Isaiah 62:11). The Great King comes with *rewards* for his people, even past saving them, further then saving them; all this and more?

It is true, that Christ by his righteousness purchased salvation for every believer and that every believer shall gain entrance into the kingdom in its consummation. He died on a cross and rose from the dead and is exalted as the Great King on his throne for every believer, and every believer will gain that entrance not by works but by faith. But the degree of capacity to happiness in heaven, was never determined by his righteousness. This is why Christ constantly talks about works and rewards in his preaching at his coming. And if rewards in the coming of the kingdom were of no value or consequence, why is the Bible filled with phrases like "pressing into the kingdom," striving, taking "the kingdom by violence"? *Why?* Is God merely speaking to hear himself talk or is there something the saints strive after for reward to be administered at Christ's glorious coming? "...the kingdom of God is preached, and every man presseth into it," (Luke 16:16). It is at his judgment that such things are passed out, at his judgment seat.

    The nations are angry with this Christ as King coming back to judge in this way. Unsaved people hate this idea of reward because *their* wages, their earned wages at the judgment *is death*, where hell follows after, and they despise the saints gaining rewards for their works. "And the nations were angry, and thy wrath is come, and the time of the dead, that they should be judged, and that thou shouldest give reward unto thy servants the prophets, and to the saints, and them that fear thy name, small and great," (Rev. 11:18). They hate this idea, and despise it; so many *professing Christians* despise it. Scripture is filled with the loveliness of this thought, that as the Spirit of God motions the Christian to serve the Great King in his kingdom for his glory while he tarries, they will be rewarded when he comes back. Their labors do not occur as vanity, as they do the wicked. The saints are rewarded for *loving God more or loving him less.* But every kingdom parable, almost every single time Jesus opens his mouth in the gospels about the kingdom, *doing* is attached to the message of the *tarrying* Owner and Master. His apostles took up this same idea constantly, "And this is love, that we walk after his commandments. This is the commandment, That, as ye have heard from the beginning, ye should walk in it. ... Look to yourselves, that we lose not those things which we have wrought, but that we receive a full reward," (2 John 1:6-8). Why? *For walking in his commandments.* A full reward is what Christians seek at the tribunal of the Great King at the Judgment. They press and strive and take the kingdom by violence for it. "Knowing that of the Lord ye shall receive the reward of the inheritance: for ye serve the Lord Christ," (Col. 3:24). As Paul explained to the Corinthians, "If any man's work abide which he hath built thereupon, he shall receive a reward. If any man's work shall be burned, he shall suffer loss: but he himself shall be saved; yet so as by fire," (1 Cor. 3:14-15). Without belaboring it, such is the constant motivation of the Spirit in the Christian to seek the kingdom, to seek the King, and his righteousness always and to "live" while they await Christ's undoubted, visible, personal, glorious, terrible and very unexpected return. The opposite is that people are scolded by the King who take their talent and stick it in the ground, procuring nothing for his kingdom where they should be expanding it. God does not zap everyone in his kingdom magically and expand it on his own, but he ordains *means* that they should walk in them; he uses means, and those means are the works of the saints by the Spirit for the good of the people of the covenant and the glory of King Jesus through the word of God.

    The Great King, in almost every single place he speaks, talks this way of heeding, and watching, and praying, and looking, and working, and striving and pressing and building and preparedness as it relates to his kingdom while he tarries;[9] judgment comes in the finality of his exaltation and highness and eternal rule, but how blessed is the Christian that is rewarded at the judgment and not condemned? "Verily there is a reward for the righteous," (Psalm 58:11). The average Christian doesn't want to speak this way; it's too much, too hard, too demanding, they think. They want these verses to read a different way, "Verily there is a reward for those saved by grace." "If any man's work abide which he hath built thereupon, it doesn't matter, he will still receive a reward anyway. For we may go on sinning that grace will abound." "If any man's work shall be burned, it doesn't matter, he will still receive a reward." "Look to yourselves, but it doesn't really matter because we will not lose anything and we will all receive a full reward at the judgment." Antinomians are very angry people that, "they should be judged, and that thou shouldest give reward unto thy servants the prophets, and to the saints, and them that fear thy

---

[9] Isa. 45:22; Mark 13:33; Luke 13:24, 16:16; Matt. 7:24; Luke 1:17, 9:62.

name, small and great;" (Rev. 11:18). They despise and hate the Great King that he speaks in this way as it pertains to the final judgment of men, and the rewards of the righteous and the rewards of the wicked. They want *no judgment seat*; and today's *counter culture* is *filled* with this idea, that you ought to receive me just like I am no matter what. Jesus will never do that. Their banner is like that theologically terrible church song, *just as I am.* No, Jesus will never accept you just as you are, instead, he says, repent, change, for the kingdom of heaven is at hand and one day all will bow before the judgement seat of the Great King to see if they have or not because he does not take people just as they are; *they must be born again.* They know deep down inside that as he rewards good, so shall he also reward evil, and this they hate. "He shall reward evil unto mine enemies:" (Psa. 54:5). "...behold and see the reward of the wicked," (Psa. 91:8). "Woe unto the wicked! it shall be ill with him: for the reward of his hands shall be given him," (Isa. 3:11). What is this Last Judgment?

Christ executes the office of his Kingship by calling out of the world a people to himself, and giving them officers, laws, and censures, by which he visibly governs them. He bestows saving grace on his elect, and yet, rewards their obedience, and corrects them for their sins, preserving and supporting them under all their temptations and sufferings, restraining and overcoming all their enemies, and powerfully ordering all things for his own glory, and their good. And he takes vengeance on the rest, who do not know God, and do not obey the gospel of his kingdom.

King Jesus requires all people who would be saved through his mercy to repent of their sins, to believe in him as the Holy Son of God and Savior, to live a holy life, and to wait on him in his own ordinances for the great day of reckoning, as the word, prayer, and sacraments, as wise virgins who take heed and are prepared, doing the work of the kingdom. Those who by the grace of God sincerely obey these precepts shall be saved, and those who willfully and finally disobey them, shall be damned in their souls after death and particular judgment, and in their bodies also, after the resurrection, and at the general and last judgment, (Mark 16:16; Romans 8:13; Matthew 25:46). All men shall rise again with their own bodies, to the last judgment: which being ended, the godly shall possess the kingdom of heaven: but unbelievers and reprobates shall be in hell tormented with the devil and his angels forever. Does this sound familiar?[10]

The end of God's appointing this day, is for the manifestation of the glory of his mercy in the eternal salvation of the elect; and of his justice in the damnation of the reprobate, who are wicked and disobedient. For then shall the righteous go into everlasting life, and receive that fulness of joy and refreshing which shall come from the presence of the Lord: but the wicked, who know not God, and do not

---

[10] See the *1647 Westminster Confession of Faith*, chapter 33.

obey the gospel of Jesus Christ, shall be cast into eternal torments, and be punished with everlasting destruction from the presence of the Lord, and from the glory of his power (as the *Confession* says).[11]

What will happen to you at the final coming of the Great King? It is certainly true that at death, he "bringeth [men] unto judgment." All the pronouncing, and executing of their sentence of absolution or condemnation occurs right there when they die as spirits. When you die, you stand before Christ the King. Later, you will stand again. For the great white throne judgement of the Great holy King will be full and general on all men, at the second coming of Christ in his exalting glory. At death you go before the King, and you go before the judgment. What is judgment but a consideration, a judging based on certain criteria for you? This criteria is based squarely on the character of God, and the law of God.[12] He will measure all men against his law. If he has saved you and you are *in* him, you will be safe. You have the white wedding garment on, and it is a very safe thing to stand before Christ wrapped in his righteousness at your judgment. But there will be a final day, in the general resurrection, where all will go before the final judgment which shall be at the last day. All men both good and bad must die

---

[11] Matt. 25:21; Rom. 9:23; Rom. 2:5-6; 9:22; 2 Thess. 1:7-8; Matt. 25:31-34; Acts 3:19; 2 Thess. 1:7; Matt. 25:41, 46; 2 Thess. 1:9.

[12] The Ten Commandments. See my work *Christ's Ten Holy Words, a Practical Study of the Ten Commandments* for a fuller discussion of this idea.

except for those that are found alive at the coming of the Son of Man, a change will occur there in them instead of death. Death, to you, if you are a saint, is a token of God's love to you, to a godly rest from all your labor and misery in this world; a mere door you walk through to go in and see the King in his courts. "Blessed are the dead which die in the Lord from henceforth: Yea, saith the Spirit, that they may rest from their labours; and their works do follow them," (Rev. 14:13). Death to the wicked is a *sting*, for they earn condemnation and judgment in the worst way after they pass through death's door. They walk into the king's courts unprepared, not having watched, and instead are rebels against his law; and they are condemned and sent to hell. While in hell, they cannot further bear the thought of later being then joined to their bodies at the final judgment, which will then be even *worse* for them, for then their bodies will suffer too, as their spirits do now. For you, as a sincere, honest, constant believer, as godly, judgment is the abolishing of sin, and perfection of putting to death the deeds of the body. For you who are wicked, sin dominates you, and the judgment is the finality of your spiritual captivity in it.

There, at the final judgment, sentence from the Great King will either be of glory or misery for those standing before him. If the Lord tarries in a far country, and does not return in our lifetime, you, reader, will be judged at the hour of your death. The King will instantly pronounce the sentence of blessing or cursing. And your soul will be then immediately conveyed into that state of happiness or misery. There you will remain until the resurrection, and from there then, both body and soul are united at the Great Judgment, and will then continue in your eternal abode forever; either for further joy or further condemnation.

The final judgment is the great day of examination for the whole world, where all men's lives that ever have been, are, or shall be, being duly examined, every one shall receive according to his works,[13] and that includes us all. Jesus Christ will come undoubtedly, personally, visibly, gloriously, and terribly to judge the world in his exalted state, breaking forth in unspeakable glory like lightning through the heavens, riding on the glory clouds, surrounded with a flame of fire, and rainbow of battle, attended with all the host of the elect angels, and especially with the voice and shout of the archangel and the trumpet of God; and so shall sit down in the royal throne of judgment to judge the nations; no one will miss the final coming of his kingdom. He will summon and present all, both the dead and living, together with angels and devils, before his glorious throne. For all men, both dead and living, shall be summoned by the voice of Christ who commands the wheels of his providence and will, and the ministry of his angels. To this, the Lord joining his divine power,

---

[13] Acts 16:31; Eccl. 12:14; 2 Cor. 5:10.

(as to the word preached for the work of the first resurrection) shall in a moment both raise the dead with their own bodies and every part of their bodies from wherever they have been scattered. He shall make them alive anew, and *fit* for eternity whether in heaven or in hell. What power is it for the Judge to call forth the bodies of the departed, that have been given over to beasts to be eaten, to the ground, to the sea, and other places, and join them eternally together, from which they have no choice but to appear? And though the elect and reprobate come before him, (in whatever way you are when the judgment comes), they shall both rise by the same mighty voice and power of Christ in the same bodies in which they lived upon earth, altered in their quality, so that they shall be able to abide forever in that state to which they will be judged; bodies specially made for heaven, and bodies specially made for hell.

By virtue of the Christ, as one elect, you will be members of his eternal body and covenant, which power is placed upon you in light of his blessed resurrection. The reprobate, they will be brought forth by virtue of the judiciary power of the King, and of the curse of the law. As elect you shall come forth to everlasting life, which is called "the resurrection of life." But if you are the reprobate, you are brought forth to shame and perpetual contempt, which is called "the resurrection of condemnation."

If you are elect, your bodies shall be spiritual, glorious, and powerful, (1 Cor. 15:42-44; Phil. 3:21), but the bodies of the reprobate shall be full of horror, terror and guilt being made answerable and fit for extreme and eternal torment. And all men shall be presented before the throne of Christ in this way, the elect being gathered by the angels, shall with great joy be caught up into the air to meet the Lord. (Luke 21:28; 1 Thess. 4:17). But, the reprobate, together with the devil and his angels, shall with extreme horror and confusion be drawn into his presence compelled to appear by force, and subject to the King in dread, (Rev. 6:15).

Then, the Great King will have these two parties separated at the judgment. The elect and reprobate are divided as his sheep that have heard his voice and followed him, on his right hand; and the reprobate goats with the devils, on the left hand, (Matt. 25:83).

There the Judge opens the books, by which the dead shall be judged, (Rev. 20:12). By the glorious illumination of Christ, the Son of Man, shining in his full strength, shall be *visibly enlightening*, that you shall perfectly remember whatever good or evil you did in the time of your life *instantly*. All the secrets of your heart will be then revealed; all you did in the heart, soul, mind and body. Such a judgment will be by *examination*, and then by *pronouncing sentence* on you. And all this will occur according to weighing the law of God against all your works.

Yet, as *the elect* of God you will not have your sins exposed, for which Christ satisfied, but only your good works will be remembered (see Hebrews 11). "All his transgressions that he hath committed, they shall not be mentioned unto him: in his righteousness that he hath done he shall live," (Ezek. 18:22). Being in Christ, you and your works will merely prove your obedience to the gospel, and partakers of the grace of the gospel. All the doubts you have now as you live as Christians are gone, and there will be no need of excuses, which you have now rolling around in your mind about how well it is with your soul; Jesus will wipe those tears away. The sentence shall be pronounced by the King himself, our Lord Jesus Christ, who, according to the evidence and verdict of conscience touching works, shall deem the elect to now have the blessing of the kingdom of God his Father because of what Christ has done in saving you, as well as what you have done in working in service to the great King. James Ussher, that famous Irish Preacher, said, "As the godly, as elect, as redeemed, you will be pronounced just, because your works, though imperfect, demonstrate your faith by which they lay hold on Christ and his meritorious righteousness, to be true faith, as working by love in all parts of obedience, (James 2:18; Gal. 5:6)."[14] And if your name is written in the Lamb's book of life (Rev. 21:27), that is, his Kingly

---

[14] Ussher, James, *A Body of Divinity*, (London: R.B. Seely and W. Burnside: 1841) 542.

decree to you his elect by God's fellow, his Mediator, this decree will be made known to all, and you will be graciously ushered into the kingdom in its fullness, rewarded then, for what you did in that state of grace while you lived here waiting for his return.

But of the wicked, if you are among the wicked with the reprobates, with the devil and his angels, he will pronounce a curse to you and that of everlasting fire. The wicked are condemned for the merit of their works, because being evil, they deserve its *wages* of hell and damnation. You see, Christians are rewarded and wicked men are rewarded, but they work in differing ways. One comes pleading the blood of Christ on all their works, another comes by working in their depravity and in rebellion against God.

By his almighty power, and the ministry of his angels, at the final judgment, the devils and reprobate men are cast into hell, and these angels will bring the King's people into the possession of his glorious kingdom. The reprobate will first be cast away, that the righteous may rejoice to see the vengeance of the King on all their oppressors; you will rejoice at that. The elect are ushered into the everlastingly blessed and glorious kingdom of the Savior who saved them by his blood and covenant. Their souls freed from all imperfections and infirmities, where even faith is made sight, and hope is made real, and repentance is now endowed with perfect wisdom and holiness. They will now, in the fullness of the kingdom, possess all the pleasures of the richness of the King in his banqueting room at the right hand of the Father, seated as princes on thrones of majesty, crowned with crowns of glory, possessing the new heaven and earth in which only righteousness dwells. You will as the elect behold and be filled with the culmination of the glorious presence of the King in his kingdom, in the company of innumerable angels and holy saints.[15] And you will then watch Christ deliver up his kingdom to the Father, and then God shall be all in all for all eternity.[16]

    This doctrine of Christ's kingdom coming in its fullness and the King coming in judgment is a terror to all graceless and wicked sinners, but a joy to the godly. What can graceless sinners find to content them in this world that will prepare them for the world to come? "All the king's servants, and the people of the king's provinces, do know, that whosoever, whether man or woman, shall come unto the king into the inner court, who is not called, there is one law of his to put him to death, except such to whom the king *shall hold out the golden sceptre*, that he may live," (Esther. 4:11). You must make haste now to come to the King while he holds out his golden scepter to you that you may repent and enter into the kingdom of heaven which is stretched out to all those seeking salvation; which are Christ's words, Christ's preaching, the truth of his kingdom. Right now

---

[15] 1 Cor. 2:9, 13:10, 12; Psalm 16:11; Rev. 3:2ff; 2 Tim. 4:8; 2 Peter 3:13; Psalm 17:15; 1 Thess. 4:17; Heb. 12:22.
[16] 1 Cor. 15:24, 28.

the Great King sees you, and you are, for all intents and purposes, standing in his court, and you seek favor in his sight: and the king holds out to you the golden scepter that is in his hand. So you draw near, and touch the top of the scepter, and the king says to you, "What wilt thou have, poor sinner, and what is thy request?" And you will answer, "That you would, O King, cleanse me, and save me, and forgive me, and preserve me, and give me power to suck the virtue of Christ's salvation day by day in all the means of grace." And the king shall say to you, "Yes, it shall be given thee, ... even the fullness of my kingdom," (consider Esther 5:2-3 in this). But it does not rest in this alone.

As the elect of God, what should you consider now who are Christians in this world as you consider the tarrying and coming of the Bridegroom, and the coming of his kingdom? Do you find in these things peace and comfort in the final judgment? What has the King done for you? He does not give you a mere gift, but the fullness of his kingdom with all its benefits. Live in expectation of his coming, then.

Have oil in your lamps as those that keep watch, and take heed, and press into the kingdom. As the King said, "Blessed is that servant, whom his lord when he cometh shall find so doing," (Luke 12:43). And he will pronounce to you the greatest words of comfort that you could ever hear, and what will that be? What are the greatest words that you could ever hear? "Well done, thou good and faithful servant: thou hast been faithful over a few things, I will make thee ruler over many things: enter thou into the joy of thy lord," (Matt. 25:21). And so, *such an entrance shall be ministered abundantly unto you into the everlasting kingdom of our Lord and Savior Jesus Christ.* Be encouraged in the undoubted, personal, visible, terrible, and glorious coming of the Savior that we may be always, "Looking unto Jesus the author and finisher of our faith," (Heb. 12:2), for the kingdom of heaven is at hand, and its fullness *could come at any time.*

Hopefully you see, then, what is further contained in these words, "Repent, for the kingdom of heaven is at hand."

Chapter 7:
The Godly Man Loves That Christ Reigns Over Him, Where the Wicked Does Not

"And I heard as it were the voice of a great multitude, and as the voice of many waters, and as the voice of mighty thunderings, saying, Alleluia: for the Lord God omnipotent reigneth," (Rev. 19:6).

We take a turn from Christ's words in Matthew 4:17 to conclude our study with Rev 19:1–8. This section of Revelation is the longest, most complex, and final song-like section in Revelation. It comes across as expressive and poetic, as well as lyrical. This lyrical section[1] has been described as a great finale to the covenant document of the establishment of Christ's rule and reign in Revelation *by way of song.* 19:1–8 consists of two divided parts: (1) 19:1–4, a two-part hymn of praise and the response, which focuses on the judgment of the whore and serves as a conclusion for the previous sections, (17:7–18:24), and, (2) in 19:5–8 there is a call to praise, *a psalm of response,* of the throne scene in 19:1–4. The theme is now turned from the obscurity of God's reign in the world, to its actual reign

---

[1] Deichgräber, Gotteshymnus, 56; Jörns, Evangelium, 144, 159, quoted by David E. Aune, *Revelation 17–22*, Volume 52C, *Word Biblical Commentary*, (Dallas: Word, Incorporated, 1998), 1021.

seen in the union of Christ and his people, *or the Lamb and his bride*, in the kingdom's final consummation.

There are three important metaphors contained in this passage: The [1] roaring of a huge crowd, [2] the roaring of the sea and [3] the voice of mighty thunder. They are linked together to emphasized the *loudness* of the sound heard; it echoes across the universe, so to speak. There is a great praise given to God's judgment of Babylon. Those praising are, "all his servants," a collective reference to, "The noise of a multitude in the mountains, like as of a great people; a tumultuous noise of the kingdoms of nations gathered together: the LORD of hosts mustereth the host of the battle," (Isa. 13:4).[2] They are the very ones whose blood was shed. They praise God for "vindicating," them. They praise God for reigning over their oppressors. These are, verse 2, "All his servants." All *believers* bear the name "servants." This echoes "Ye that fear the LORD, trust in the LORD: he is their help and their shield," (Psa. 115:11), and those "small and great," defines, "those who fear him," as in Rev. 11:18, "all his servants, those fearing him, the small and the great." They proclaim and sing the song *very loud.* They sing against the heathen, and for the rule of God over all things. Why? "...because the Lord God Almighty has begun to reign," (ἐβασίλευσεν).

---

[2] See G. K. Beale, *The Book of Revelation: A Commentary on the Greek Text*, New International Greek Testament Commentary, (Grand Rapids, MI; Carlisle, Cumbria: W.B. Eerdmans; Paternoster Press, 1999), 933.

Christ shows himself to be the all-powerful divine King by this great act of overthrowing the wicked. "The kingdom of the earth has come to be transferred to our Lord and his Messiah, and he will reign forever and ever," (Rev. 11:15). This section is a development of chapter 11 is clear from its restatement of a section of 11:17, "Saying, We give thee thanks, O Lord God Almighty, which art, and wast, and art to come; because thou hast taken to thee thy great power, and hast reigned," (Rev. 11:17).

The phrase "the sound of much water" is attributed to the four cherubim in Ezek. 1:24, but in Ezek. 43:2 the same Hebrew phrase is interpreted as "a voice of a host" (παρεμβολή), "And when they went, I heard the noise of their wings, like the noise of great waters, as the voice of the Almighty, the voice of speech, as the noise of an host: when they stood, they let down their wings," (Ezek. 1:24).[3] Angels and men crying out in praise of the great King. κύριος ἐβασίλευσεν (the Lord reigned) is extensive through the psalms. This shows that God establishes his visible kingship after judging the church's enemies. Zech. 14:9 and Rev. 19:6 use the same expression to speak of the eschatological (end times) future, when God will again establish his kingship universally on earth after defeating his enemy, a future of which all accounts in the psalms were hints of and finalized at the coming of the King.

---

[3] *Ibid*, Beale.

Exod. 15:17–18 can also be alluded to where the Red Sea victory is the basis for the church's future possession of the Promised Land and God's reign there in his good news. And what is this gospel they sing of from the time of the Exodus to the time of the prophets? "How beautiful upon the mountains are the feet of him that bringeth good tidings, that publisheth peace; that bringeth good tidings of good, that publisheth salvation; that saith unto Zion, Thy God reigneth!" (Isa. 52:7). "I will greatly rejoice in the LORD, my soul shall be joyful in my God; for he hath clothed me with the garments of salvation, he hath covered me with the robe of righteousness, as a bridegroom decketh himself with ornaments, and as a bride adorneth herself with her jewels," (Isa. 61:10). "Reigneth" is literally, "reigned." He has *reigned now once for all*. His reign is a fact established, and now *proclaimed* in Revelation.

Babylon, the harlot, was one great hindrance to his reign being recognized. He overthrows all that is comprehended in the term "harlot."[4] All spiritual adulteries are overcome by the blood of the Lamb, and he is fully revealed in his reign. Revelation 19:11–22:5 surrounds Christ's return; his certain, personal, visible, glorious and terrible return, the one that is very unexpected. In the end of Revelation is found the

---

[4] Robert Jamieson, A. R. Fausset, and David Brown, *Commentary Critical and Explanatory on the Whole Bible*, Volume 2, (Oak Harbor, WA: Logos Research Systems, Inc., 1997), 596.

second coming of Christ (19:11–16), the defeat of the Antichrist (19:17–21), the binding of Satan (20:1–3), the kingdom of Christ (20:4–6), the loosing of Satan and his final defeat (20:7–10), the last judgment at the great white throne (20:11–15), and the new heavens and new earth (21:1–22:5). All this is part of Christ's final exaltation. But these 10 verses in chapter 19 show Christ as prophetically reigning and ruling over his people, and the whole world. Christ became King in the fulness of his power on earth ruling over the fall and all world powers, and does so from his exaltation, beginning at his resurrection and into the ages, to be consummated when he comes back. Now, here at the end, his reign is *universally recognized*, and he rules over all, in all places, in heaven and hell, in his exaltation, from the throne of power. It is spoken by his servants, his disciples, his redeemed, who declare he reigns, who declare his gospel, *Our God Reigns*. This is the shout and song of all the godly; and they love him for it; Alleluia: for the Lord God omnipotent reigneth!

What shall we consider here? The godly man *loves* that Christ reigns over him, where the wicked does not. Considering what has been taught so far about God as King and his kingdom, we have considered the following: 1) God Reigns as King both absolutely as the Royal King over the whole earth, and particularly as Redeemer and Savior of his church. 2) *Our God Reigns* through his Christ for his glory in his kingdom; this was the substance of Christ's preaching.

3) Repentance is required to enter into the kingdom of heaven, and to receive it. 4) God's particular reign as King is expressed in Christ's substitutionary atonement and its application to penitent and believing sinners. 5) Christ's particular reign as King is over his church through his atonement as seen in the Lord's Supper, a visible expression of his word. We used that as an example of a summation of all his benefits to us. 6) Christ's reign as King over his church and the world is finalized in the Last Judgment when he shall come undoubtedly, personally, visibly, gloriously, terribly and very unexpectedly, and we are to live in a certain manner now while he tarries.

We consider in this final chapter, that *all this* makes his people *very happy*. Christ is this elect Servant who embodies the message that God reigns supreme both in his absolute dominion over all people, and in saving his own special people. Servants do the praising in God's dominion and kingdom. The Christ, the Anointed one, is exalted *in* their praises. He will be praised very high by them. The thoughts they have of him are very high thoughts; lofty thoughts; he must increase and they must decrease. He is sent to fulfill the *covenant* of God and preaches the coming of this kingdom in his delivery of this message all through the gospels. "Thy God reigns" is the message (embodying everything about the crucified Messiah), and the exaltation of the servant of God expresses this message of this good news, tidings which shall be for all the people. This is because all godly men love that Christ reigns over them for his glory. This implies many things in it, but we will only consider *four of them*. I use the phrase *godly men*, as a phrase covering converted male and female, young and old, whom Christ has graciously saved.

[1] The godly man loves that Christ reigns absolutely over everything. Scripture teaches that God is sovereign over everything, and the godly man loves this. God's sovereign governance extends to everything. The godly man loves that God is sovereign over the entire universe, (Psa. 103:19; Rom. 8:28; Eph. 1:11). He loves that God is sovereign over all of nature, (Psa. 135:6-7; Matt. 5:45; 6:25-30). He loves that God is sovereign over angels and Satan, (Psa. 103:20-21; Job 1:12). He loves that God is sovereign over nations, (Psa. 47:7-9; Dan. 2:20-21; 4:34-35). He loves that God is sovereign over human beings, (1 Sam. 2:6-7; Gal. 1:15-16). He loves that God is sovereign over animals, (Psa. 104:21-30; 1 Kings 17:4-6). He loves that God is sovereign over things that seem to be an accident, (Prov. 16:33; John 1:7; Matt. 10:29). He loves that God is sovereign over free acts of men, (Exod. 3:21; 12:25-36; Ezek. 7:27). He loves that God is sovereign over sinful acts of men and even of Satan, (2 Sam. 24:1; 1 Chron. 21:1; Gen 45:5; 50:20). The godly man loves this because he knows men have no power in the world even to change one hair on their head from black to white. The godly man has no power to change his hair instantly

upon his immediate desire. There are very few if any things that he can really do in that way, and he knows it. The godly man knows he is a servant to the divine will. The godly man knows our God is in the heavens and he does whatsoever he pleases. The godly man loves that God has an absolute, independent right of disposing of all creatures according to his own pleasure. The godly man is pleased that God is so powerful, and unchangeably so. He praises God for this, in fact, he praises God into eternity for this fact. *Alleluia: for the Lord God omnipotent reigneth* is his banner.

    The wicked *hate* that God reigns. Christ said of the world, "but me it hateth, because I testify of it, that the works thereof are evil," (John 7:7). They do not want God to reign over them; and they do not want God's Christ to tell them what to do; in fact, many professing Christians act like the wicked when they hate that God reigns over everything. "Reprove not a scorner, lest he hate thee," (Prov. 9:8). The wicked hate that God tells them what to do. They hate that God requires them to follow his will. They hate the only means and manner of finding true happiness because their minds and hearts are darkened by sin and Satan. They hate Christ, and hate to acknowledge him, "let them also that hate him flee before him," (Psa. 68:1). When Christ came to earth incarnate, came to save in human flesh, they hated him so much they nailed him to a cross and killed him. Jesus Christ was murdered. He was first beaten to the breadth of his human life, then stripped naked and humiliated verbally and physically, abandoned by his disciples, forced to walk naked publicly to carry his cross to the place of execution, nailed to it, and then was given over to death being abandoned by the Father. God sovereignly ordained *every bit of it* and the godly man *loves* Jesus for all this. His *salvation* is found within the propositions of those truths. God sovereignly ordained the most horrific crime in history (where all other trials, afflictions and difficulties in the life of a human man pale in comparison) and God did this to his Son in the most unpleasant way possible, for his glory and the godly man's good. "[Christ], being delivered by the determinate counsel and foreknowledge of God, ye have taken, and by wicked hands have crucified and slain," (Acts 2:23). The godly man loves that God sovereignly ordained the most atrocious murder in all of history, and he used sinful men to accomplish his glorifying ends. Why, but that the godly man receives a great benefit in this work, and knows that without such a death, and such a glorious resurrection by God's Messiah, that his own heart would never be raised up from the dead to serve the living God. The godly man loves that Christ reigns absolutely over everything.

[2] The godly man loves that Christ reigns over him personally, and reigns in his heart. This internal government, this reigning over men, is *monergistic* in salvation; the godly man loves this, and the wicked man hates this. In other words, God changes sinners

sovereignly into saints by endowing them with a spiritual principle foreign to them, something he gives them, and something he blesses them with and by. This is something they did not have, could not create or fabricate, for God's Spirit gives it to them. He blows where he wills, and when he wills; for it is not by their will, they have no power over one hair on their head. In fact, all those who try to claim that power for themselves rob Christ of his glory in it.[5]

    God reigns over the hearts of men. Like rivers of water he turns the King's heart, president's hearts, men's hearts, wherever he wishes, and the godly man loves that. What godly man doesn't love that? It must be this way because the right of governing men's consciences belongs to none but Christ, who is both infinitely wise and most powerful by the Spirit to change sinners into saints. Christ has no underling that does this for him, he does it directly, through his unbounded Spirit, by the infinite power of the Godhead. It must necessarily be of infinite power to change the heart of the wicked man into the heart of a godly man, into a saint. What does "saint" mean but to be set apart? And who does this setting apart? The godly man knows that his heart was so black with darkness and hate for God, only the light of God could change it, replace it, and renew it. But this the godly man loves, and knows intimately this truth, for God has

---

[5] See my work *John 3:16 Second Edition* for a full discussion of this principle.

promised to reveal the secrets of his covenant to his people, to those he changes into new men. How can one be changed or saved without the gospel of the kingdom? It is *impossible*, and the godly man knows this. The throne of an unsaved man, and unconverted man, is set in all kinds of selfish and worldly pursuits; and allows, unknown to the sinner, that throne of his heart to be occupied by their father the devil. The wicked, they think they rule and reign in their heart, and they are determined to be masters of their own destiny. But they *serve* the kingdom of darkness. They serve the god of this world, the king of darkness.[6] They serve the world and its pursuits which sit diametrically opposed to God's kingdom. They serve themselves – this is self-love, or idolatry. They are slaves to wickedness, and are so entrenched in it that they are described as "dead men" by Scripture, (Eph.2:1) ... dead in sin. They are, for all intents and purposes, walking zombies that must be reanimated by the infinite power of Christ's Spirit. "...he that raised up Christ from the dead shall also quicken your mortal bodies by his Spirit that dwelleth in you," (Rom. 8:11). Such a spiritually dead disposition must be conquered and overthrown by King Jesus; this the godly man knows to be true. "For he must reign, till he hath put all enemies under his feet. The last enemy that shall be destroyed is death," (1 Cor. 15:25-26). And how shall this enemy of death be conquered? "...you he hath quickened..." (Eph. 2:1). What an infinitely

---

[6] John 8:44; 1 John 3:8.

powerful Jesus he is to change a dead man into a living man. To change a stony heart into a beating heart (Ezekiel 11:19, 36:26).

The shout of the godly is, "the Lord God omnipotent reigneth," over everything, including my heart. "And I will give them one heart, and I will put a new spirit within you; and I will take the stony heart out of their flesh, and will give them an heart of flesh," (Ezek. 11:19). The godly man *loves* this. He loves that Christ rules over his heart, personally. He loves that Christ by his Spirit gives his heart new dispositions. He loves that the Spirit has sovereign entrance and glorious power over his heart. He loves the new spiritual principle given to him by the power of God. He does not mind that God rules his heart at all, in fact, he prefers it, and he even wishes that God would rule more of his heart more of the time. He knows he has been changed from death to life, and he knows that the sovereignty and power of Christ has accomplished this. That he is in fact born from above. He is happy for this, for the godly man loves that Christ reigns over him personally, and reigns in his heart.

[3] The godly man will not glory in himself but in Christ; he *loves* to do this. The godly man exalts Christ both inwardly and outwardly. Inwardly in his heart, soul and mind. "Thou shalt love the Lord thy God with all thy heart, and with all thy soul, and with all thy mind," (Matt. 22:37). The godly man knows that all his worth is the worth of Christ in him, and all his

blessedness comes from Christ. The godly man is happy to be poor in spirit (Matt. 5:3). The godly man is happy to mourn (Matt. 5:4). The godly man is happy to be meek (Matt. 5:5). The godly man is happy to hunger and thirst after righteousness (Matt. 5:6). The godly man is happy to be persecuted for righteousness' sake (Matthew 5:10), for they know in this they belong to the kingdom of heaven. "Not unto us, O LORD, not unto us, but unto thy name give glory, for thy mercy, and for thy truth's sake," (Psa. 115:1). The godly man's heart is abased for Christ, it is happily so. Even so much that all the glory belongs to Christ alone. There is no room for their own glory; and they love that God takes up all the glory in every way.

This is a testimony to the godly man's happy disposition. As much as inwardly, so as outwardly, with the entirety of his bodily parts and all strength. "That, according as it is written, He that glorieth, let him glory in the Lord," (1 Cor. 1:31). He does this with *all* his parts. He does this with *all* his strength. He does it with his eyes, in what he will see, with his ears, in what we he will hear, with his hands with what he will handle, with his feet in taking him far away from sin. All his parts are used to glorify Christ and he loves this. Simply, the godly man is humbled before Christ in what he is and what he does. In what he is, he knows he is a sinner. "Likewise, I say unto you, there is joy in the presence of the angels of God over one sinner that repenteth," (Luke 15:10).

The godly man knows he was like this, being a repentant sinner, and so he is happy to be found by the Christ *repenting* as his lifestyle. He knows he is a worm. "How much less man, that is a worm? and the son of man, which is a worm?" (Job 25:6). The godly man is humbled in that, not offended; he doesn't mind giving Christ all the glory in taking a worm like he is and making him a saint. He is humbled in what he does. In service to God. "...for ye serve the Lord Christ," (Col. 3:24). He knows that Christ is the Messiah, but the godly man knows he is the Lord that is all powerful, and reigns, and is happy to be in service to him regardless of the service offered. "I had rather be a doorkeeper in the house of my God, than to dwell in the tents of wickedness," (Psa. 84:10), David said. He will serve Christ according to God's will. "...according to the will of God and our Father," (Gal. 1:4).

And the godly man knows that "if we ask any thing according to his will, he heareth us," (1 John 5:14). So anything he needs in his service to the great King will be heard and spiritual power will be given making him suitable to the work. He knows it is not his power, but Christ's power, Christ's almighty power, and is happy in this that God is so able on his behalf. He will remain in service to God in worship all his days. "Wherefore we receiving a kingdom which cannot be moved, let us have grace, whereby we may serve God acceptably with reverence and godly fear," (Heb. 12:28).

The godly man knows this service is very reasonable because of what Christ has done for him, and so orders his own life accordingly, "that ye present your bodies a living sacrifice, holy, acceptable unto God, which is your reasonable service," (Rom. 12:1). In everything, the godly man knows that his whole life surrounds this basic premise: that the godly man will not glory in himself but in Christ, in everything, and he loves to do this.

[4] The godly man will praise Christ for who he is and what he does, and enthrones the King in his praises and exaltation of his glorious character. "But thou art holy, O thou that inhabitest the praises of Israel," (Psa. 22:3). Jesus is the God-man, Christ is God and man, sitting at the Father's right hand. He is God equal with the Father, and the Holy Spirit. "For in him dwelleth all the fulness of the Godhead bodily," (Col. 2:9), and this the godly man rejoices in. The godly man is happy that God came among men, and drew near to man in his incarnation. That Christ is God with us, God and man by a personal union of both natures; and the servant of God, by an astonishing condescension of grace, (1 Cor. 11:3) came *near*.

Jesus Christ is the man that is God's *fellow*. He is the one who has the nearest and most intimate acquaintance with God. "Awake, O sword, against my shepherd, and against the man that is *my fellow*, saith the LORD of hosts," (Zech. 13:7). The godly man loves that Christ in the word is declared to be King of the saints, head of all principalities and powers, exalted above every name that is named in this world, and in the world to come as the God-man; he loves that Christ is the delight of God's soul. Isa. 42:1 says, "Behold my servant, whom I uphold; mine elect, in whom my soul delighteth; I have put my spirit upon him: he shall bring forth judgment to the Gentiles." Now, the godly man who loves this reigning Christ says of this blessed Mediator, "This my beloved, and this is my friend. God has highly exalted him; and highly do I exalt him. *The Lord God omnipotent reigneth*; this is my Jesus. It is the Father's will, and (*through his grace*) it is as truly my will; that all men should honor him, even as they honor the Father. And that they confess him to be their Lord, to the honor of the Father, who is honored in their honoring of him, and dishonored in their dishonoring of him, this Mediator is my Lord, and I will worship him," and the godly man loves to do so with divine worship. He loves the great reigning King.

  The godly man loves that the Mediator is God, as well as man; and to his divine excellency is due the utmost divine worship by him. The godly man thinks to himself, "Him will I esteem above all; and count all things but loss and dung for the excellency of the knowledge of King Christ Jesus. In him will I believe. I do believe in God the Father. I will believe in Christ no less. And so also the Spirit of Christ. Him will I love. I am content, that grace is to none but such as love the Lord Jesus Christ in sincerity. Him will I love in sincerity, him will I give reverence and obey; as charged by God to listen to him, obey his voice, not provoke him; because God's name is in me. Him will I worship in the house of God, and in all ordinances will I draw near to him, who alone has power to encourage my happiness. He is the Great King, and I love him as such." He loves him as Redeemer and Deliverer. The godly man loves Christ as Redeemer and Deliverer, and says, "I love this Mediator, and he is my meditation every day. Who is the Christ that is, a Savior from sin and all the curses of sin? Who is Redeemer; that is, as to the manner of his saving, one who saves by the payment of a valuable price, even invaluable? Who is the Deliverer and Mediator to be in the middle of God offended and of me offending? He is the one who stands in a middle place between God and me, whom sin had set at odds; where I was at war with God before, but no longer. There I find him, laboring, to reconcile me to God, by a satisfactory price, and to reconcile me to God by a victorious power. This power he could not have had, if he had not been God; and which price he could not have paid, if he had not been both God and man. He is my Surety, the one who satisfies my debt, and performs the covenant for me. He is white and ruddy and altogether lovely, God and man, while my Redeemer and Deliverer." In all this, the godly man loves that Christ reigns over him, where the wicked man does not.

If you are a godly person, reader, you *love* that Christ rules over your heart and life. You love that Christ enforces his will and law on you, and you pray that his will would be done in you and for you; you pray for his will to be done. He looks for you to be careful in your obedience to it, but you love to be obedient to him. Matthew 11:29, "Take my yoke upon you, and learn of me." You are happy to do that, happy to learn. We find in this that he desires of you as a godly person to be careful in your obedience to it, but it is not bondage. You know very well he has delivered you from the bondage of the law as a slave. He has made you free, and you are happy to say to him, "the Lord God omnipotent reigneth over me." Obedience for you is a *pleasure* now, and self-denial, carrying your cross for him, is *easy*. You are happy to do it.

Before you were converted you were always very wicked and naughty. "For we ourselves also were sometimes foolish, disobedient, deceived, serving divers lusts and pleasures, living in malice and envy, hateful, and hating one another." And then what happened? "But after that the kindness and love of God our Saviour toward man appeared, not by works of righteousness which we have done, but according to his mercy he saved us, by the washing of regeneration, and renewing of the Holy Ghost; which he shed on us abundantly through Jesus Christ our Saviour; That being justified by his grace, we should be made heirs according to the hope of eternal life," (Titus 3:3-7).

Chapter 7: The Godly Man Loves that Christ Reigns as King

You know that his, "His commandments are not grievous." You are happy when he corrects you, and thankful when he rebukes and chastises you for your sin, and you love him for it. You are happy that, "whom he loves he rebukes and chastens," (Heb. 12:6-7). You are happy he takes notice. You know there are many parents who do not take notice of their children, do not discipline them. You are happy that God follows your every thought, and every step and corrects you as needs be. Does not the Psalmist say, "Thy rod and thy staff, they comfort me," (Psalm 23:3). You are very happy that he does this, and will oblige willingly that he rules over you as such. The wicked, he allows them to go on stubbornly in the way of their own hearts. You are very happy he does not do that with you. You know that Christ will spend no time with the wicked for their good, but all that he does for you is for you good. You are very happy in this, and you love him for it.

You, as a godly person love that Christ protects you in ways you don't even know he does. He will not allow you to fall into a way of sin and bondage to Satan anymore; and keeps you from so many sins. Satan is always taking note of the *hedge of protection* around you. He sees what God is doing, as with the hedge God made around Job.[7] You may not be aware of this, as Job was not, but you are happy for God's protection in all he does; even in a general way. But doesn't God do more for you than you can imagine? You are happy he

---
[7] Job 1:10.

does, and you love from that. Jesus says in John 17:12, "All that thou hast given me I have kept, and none of them is lost..." He cannot lose you if he has given himself for you. You love him especially for *that* too. You are kept by God's hands, by the omnipotent hand of the God who reigns, and you love him for that and are very happy he has come to you and made himself known to you and preserves you from all that could be dread and fear and terrible for the wicked. You are among those who believe and are, "preserved in Christ Jesus," (Jude 1:1).

You well know that it is never your own strength or grace that protects you, but only Christ's omnipotent power that does it. It is his care, attention, charge, supervision, and continual watchfulness that keeps you safe, and you love him for it. This is his covenant with you, Jer. 32:4, "I will put my fear in their hearts, that they shall not depart from me." He preserves you from all fear, and no longer gives you a spirit of fear, but of power, love and a sound mind. You see beloved, this you know. You have a sound mind for it. You experience his love for you in it.

You as a godly person love that Christ reigns omnipotently over your whole life, even that he rewards your obedience to him; which is an unfathomable thought atop many other unfathomable spiritual thoughts. He encourages you in your good works by rewarding you for them. You love that he has placed his Spirit in you, to will and to do according to his good pleasure. You are very happy that he has put his Spirit there to lead and guide you and help you in everything. And yet you love that he encourages such sincere service from you that all you do, you do for Christ in comfort and happiness because of God's preserving power.

You love that God is a, "bountiful rewarder of such as diligently seek him," (Heb. 11:6). You love that God has *made you a diligent seeker*. You love that he is such a gracious King who extends to you not only talents for service, not only pounds to make more, to gain more responsibility before him, but that he extends the grace of his golden scepter that you might come into his courts with praise and thanksgiving in all your service; and he is willing to give you a kingdom.

The wicked see God as a hard taskmaster, and rightly so. They want to say with Pharaoh, "I know not the Lord...who is God that I should obey his voice?"[8] yet they censor his truth in their sin and do not do those things which would bring them true happiness. They complain of such a hard life without God, and seek only sinful pleasures; thinking they will be of some help and comfort in their misery. Have you any reason to complain of Christ's service as a *godly* person? No, you as a godly person *love* all that Christ commands you as *the omnipotent Lord that reigns*.

---

[8] Exodus 5:2.

You love that he comforts you, and makes life easy in his service knowing that he makes good, even, come out of the evil of affliction. You love that he commands peace towards you, which "rules in" your hearts, (Col. 3:15) no matter what your trials might be. He reigns powerfully for your comfort, infinitely so, regardless of the circumstances. But you know all is in his power. He is omnipotent, all powerful, and he reigns, and you love that he does. Nothing takes him by surprise. His kingdom is not mere talk for you, as it is with those who wallow in their hypocrisy, and you love that, "his kingdom is not in word, but in power," (1 Cor. 4:20), and you experience that power in the preaching of his word and in his truth. He rules you and draws you to service this way, Hosea 11:4, "I drew them with the cords of a man, with bands of love," and you love him for it.

As a godly person you love to submit under the omnipotent power of the Christ and his reign. You will not, "have fellowship with the unfruitful works of darkness;" you will not, "walk in the counsel of the wicked, nor stand in the way of sinners." You will not hang out with or put up with, "workers of iniquity," (Psalm 1:1, 26; 2 Corinthians 6); as a godly person, you don't do that.

You will afflict and humble your soul for your sins, mourning and weeping for them, until the Lord is pleased to show mercy and forgive you. You account your sins to be your greatest burden. You cannot make a mockery of sin knowing it is a great wickedness against God. You will labor to be holy in all parts of your conversation, watching over your own ways at all times, and in all companies, (Psalm 50:23, Isaiah 56:8, 2 Peter 3), and love to do it, are happy to do it for Christ's glory.

You will make a conscience effort of the least of his commandments as well as the greatest, avoiding filthy speaking and vain talking, as much as whoredom; lesser oaths as well as greater; evil talk, as well as violent actions.[9]

You love and esteem, and labor to be affected by the preaching of the word, above all earthly treasures, knowing Christ's voice is found there; and you love to see him there. You love to hear the great omnipotent King reign in his word in your heart.

You honor the godly, and delight in the company of such as truly fear God, above all others, (Psalm 15).

You are careful in the sanctification of his Sabbath; neither daring to violate that holy rest by labor, nor to neglect the holy duties belonging to God's service public or private, (Isaiah 56 and 58).

You do not love the world, neither the things of it, but you wholeheartedly are affected in things that concern a better life.

---

[9] Byfield, Nicholas, *The Signs of a Wicked Man and the Signs of a Godly Man*, (Coconut Creek, FL: Puritan Publications, 2013) eBook, section Chapter 1: Describing the Godly Man by Such Signs as Discover Him to The Observation of Other Men.

You live in the profession of the sincerity of the gospel, and do such duties as you know God requires of you in the business of your soul, making religion your chief interest, notwithstanding the oppositions of all profane people, or where carnal friends will dislike you for; for you love Christ above all other things.

You strive to be more godly this week than last, and strive to enter in at the straight gate, taking the kingdom by violence and besieging the castle of Christ's will by force.

You set up a daily course of serving God, and that with your family too, if you have any; and exercise yourself in the word of God, as the chief joy of your heart, and the daily refuge of your life, calling on the omnipotence of Christ continually, for your good; and in all this, you, as a godly person, love the Lord Jesus Christ in sincerity. And over your whole life your banner is "the Lord God omnipotent reigneth," and this you love, because it is the gospel, and the substance of Christ's preaching.

In contrast, how great is their sin and misery who continue in bondage to sin and Satan, and refuse the government of Christ who reigns omnipotently. They would rather sit under the shadow of the devil than under the sweet and powerful government of the light of Christ. If you are still a servant of the devil, you are in a terrible plight. Satan enslaves those of you who do not serve the Christ. He has written down his service in your blood. He chains you with severe bondage to sin. He rules you with cruel oppression. He rewards all your faithful work to his kingdom with everlasting damnation and misery.

How long does it take for the ungodly to hear, to turn to repent without delay? *It is very hard.* But Christ will receive all poor sinners to himself, and save them, and will lose none that come to him by faith. It may be that you think that you do not know who's reign you sit under. Is it not then important to find this out? Make a trial of it and consider it. Who is king over your soul? Who is on the throne of your heart, Christ or Satan? Where is your obedience? To whom do you yield to each day?

As a godly person, you love the *infinite love* of Christ as the crucified one, he who was dead and came alive by omnipotent resurrection to save poor souls and make them happy under his supreme rule. You love that Christ is the master of life and death. He, the immutable God who holds time and space in the palm of his hand, the one who is without limits in his character and being, the one who controls the time of their life and the time of their death, and subsequently, orders such godly lives for his glory and their happiness. Such words should give you hope, and make you rejoice as a godly person. Because of the redemptive act of the crucifixion and resurrection, Christ has secured your victory over the devil, death and saved you from the wrath of God (1 Thess. 1:10).

You who serve Satan now, serve Satan no longer. Christ is the victorious one, and he promises that all those who submit to his rule and reign are in fact victorious as well, in fact, more than conquerors in Christ Jesus. Heaven awaits them whether they die now by the hands of persecution, or later by natural causes – which are both by God's omnipotent and sovereign appointment. But salvation is only found through the immutable, incarnate, crucified and risen Christ, whom the godly praise and shout with all manner of love to him because he reigns. And all godly people love this Christ who reigns over them, where all the wicked do not.

The godly delight in seeing Christ exalted. They love to see Christ reigning on the throne of his glory, exalted on high. They love to have him do whatever his will is and whatever his pleasure is in and among the inhabitants of the earth. They love that he should do just what he pleases. Do you? This is the kingdom, kingship, dominion, rule, governing, through repentance, by his substitutionary atonement, for the glory of the Father, and all our spiritual benefits of believing in him, concerning the kingdom, that *the Lord God omnipotent reigneth*, which shall be proclaimed by the saints into eternity, which Christ came preaching in times past, as do all his commissioned heralds at this present time preach.

May we understand the preaching of the kingdom, for the practical outworking of all that we have studied about God's kingdom in this way, for the godly man loves that Christ reigns over him in such a holy reign and in such a holy kingdom, *where the wicked does not.*

FINIS

Other Helpful Books Published by Puritan Publications

Consider some of Dr. McMahon's other works:

John 3:16, Second Edition
5 Marks of a Biblical Church
5 Marks of Biblical Commitment to the Visible Body of Christ
5 Marks of a Biblical Disciple
5 Marks of Biblical Reformation
5 Marks of Christian Resolve
5 Marks of Devotion to God
A Practical Guide to Primeval History
Augustine's Calvinism
Christ Commanding His Coronavirus to Covenant Breakers
Eternity Weighed in the Balance
Covenant Theology Made Easy
Historical Theology Made Easy
How to Live Every Day in the End Times
Joseph's Resolve and the Unreasonableness of Sinning Against God
Seeing Christ Clearly
Systematic Theology Made Easy
The Five Principles of the gospel
The Two Wills of God Made Easy
The Reformed Apprentice, a Workbook on Reformed Theology
The Reformation Made Easy

Also, consider these newly published puritan works:

A Call to Delaying Sinners
by Thomas Doolittle (1632–1707)

A Treatise of the Loves of Christ to His Spouse
by Samuel Bolton, D.D. (1606-1654)

Attending the Lord's Table
by Henry Tozer (1602-1650)

Faith, Election and the Believer's Assurance
by George Gifford (1547-1620)

God is Our Refuge and Our Strength
by George Gipps (n.d.)

Remembering Your Creator
by Matthew Mead (Mead) (1630-1699)

Resisting the Devil with a Steadfast Faith
by George Gifford (1547-1620)

Taking Hold of Eternal Life in Christ
by George Gifford (1547-1620)

The Believer's Marriage with Christ
by Michael Harrison (1640-1729)

The Kingdom of Heaven is Upon You

The Blessed God
by Daniel Burgess (1645-1713)

The Doctrine of Man's Future Eternity
by John Jackson (1600-1648)

The Victorious Christian Soldier in Christ's Army
by Urian Oakes (1631–1681)

Zeal for God's House Quickened
by Oliver Bowles B.D. (1574-1664?)

www.ingramcontent.com/pod-product-compliance
Lightning Source LLC
Chambersburg PA
CBHW050524170426
43201CB00013B/2078